ATTACK TRANSPORT
THE STORY OF THE U.S.S. DOYEN

LAWRENCE A. MARSDEN
Lieutenant, Supply Corps, United States Navy

TABLE OF CONTENTS

Foreword

Among the auxiliary classes of the Navy List are two that carry not only an "auxiliary" but also a "combatant" classification letter. These are the attack transports (APA's) and the attack cargo vessels (AKA's) . Without belittling the importance of LST's, LSM's, LCT's, and other small types used in the maritime transportation of men and freight, it is the APA's and the AKA's that carry the bulk of the troops and equipment to the bloody assault beaches of our overseas landings. They are the backbone of the Amphibious Forces. These ships arrive with the initial amphibious attacks and continue their support throughout the fighting. Unarmored and with small fire power, they yet carry a great weapon that is war's one essential combat element: the troops that fight on the ground.

In war, transports seldom rest. Between assaults, on long and dreary voyages they carry out to distant bases replacement and service troops and freight, and carry back to home ports our casualties and essential war materials. They are the unsung, battle-scarred work horses of the Navy.

The men of the ships' companies (chiefly naval, but with a small percentage of Coast Guard) who manned the APA's and the AKA's during the war were mostly Reserves, with a small nucleus of Regulars. Because the operation of these types was new to us, the men of the transports in commission at the beginning of the war necessarily learned their highly technical duties by experience. Drafts from the older vessels provided nuclei of officers and bluejackets as the foundations on which new vessels could build effective organizational structures. Consequently, experience was at a premium. All vessels had many new men in their ships' companies. A transport that had been through one amphibious operation was a veteran.

Transport life was mainly on a humdrum level that had occasional peaks of furious battle. Morale was always high. The resourceful crews of these ships made up for lack of experience through native ingenuity, shining courage, and an eager offensive spirit.

As modestly portrayed in Attack Transport, these truly combatant naval vessels of the Amphibious Forces did their share in winning the war.

God bless them and the splendid Americans who worked and fought them!

Richmond K. Turner

Admiral, US. Navy, Former Commander Amphibious Forces, Pacific Fleet

New York City

April 11, 1946

A Word from the Author

How did this book come to be written? That is the question, I understand, that all prefaces should answer.

I wish that I could give an unusual reason, or at least an original one, but I can't. Attack Transport was written partly for something to do and partly as a memento for the men who served on the Doyen.

It was just after the Iwo Jima operation, when the ship was en route to Guam, that the work was actually begun. The original plan was to trace the action of the Doyen from commissioning through her last operation.

Getting the material wasn't easy. Since I reported aboard just before the Saipan invasion, I had no personal knowledge of the commissioning ceremony, or of the Kiska, Gilbert, or Marshall Islands campaigns. All the facts and incidents had to be drawn laboriously from the old-timers aboard — the "plank owners" they were called. But it was done, and the words were at last set down on paper.

The story is told in the first person throughout, as if I had been on the scene from the time the ship was commissioned. I have taken this liberty with the facts, not to claim credit for actions in which I did not participate, but simply and wholly in the interests of producing a smoother and more personal narrative.

Though I did not actually report aboard until after the Marshalls, the factual material preceding that time is true. All the incidents happened, and the characters involved took part in them. The chapter on crossing the equator is wholly authentic. The Doyen crossed the line at least eight times. I have merely transposed my own initiation experiences to a crossing of an earlier date.

Attack Transport professes to do but one thing — to describe the war in the Pacific as it was seen from one small unit of the fleet. It is not an analytical discussion of policies, but merely an account of the day-to-day life. Combat has been kept in its proper relation to other activities.

It is not the story of one man, or essentially of one ship. It is a compilation of the experiences of many of our ship's personnel; it represents many hours of bull sessions — of long discussions with Commander Hogan, Doc Gil, Doc Watkins, Doc Kelly, Tom Hawk, Ed

Buczek, Sal Murino, Cliff Hanlin, "Pop" Slattery, "Ace" Parker, and the many others who are all its indirect authors. The experiences were not peculiar to the Doyen. They have been duplicated on the hundreds of other vessels of the Amphibious Force with which we traveled. I sincerely hope that the book is worthy of the men and the ship it describes.

Lawrence A. Marsden
Washington
January 1946

1. A Fighting Ship is Born

It was on a Monday morning that I received my orders to report for sea duty. The regular routine of the week was just beginning when the telephone on my desk rang. The voice of the skipper boomed over the wire. "Larry, start packing your bags — you're going to sea!" The skipper quoted: ". . . upon detachment you will proceed and report to the Commanding Officer of the U.S.S. Doyen (APA-1)."

Whatever kind of ship APA-1 was, it certainly had a low number. No one in the office had ever heard of APA's, but the war was still young and ignorance of new fleet units wasn't at all unusual. Finally we unearthed an antiquated ship classification list. I opened it to the A's. Down the list . . . "AP — Troop Transport" . . . and almost at the bottom . . . "APA — Animal Transport."

Animal transport! I could see myself as jockey on a seagoing freight car, or perhaps "stable boy" would be a more accurate term. I closed the pamphlet and stuffed it into my lowest desk drawer. Bad enough to suffer ignominy alone ... no reason to share it with an unsympathetic office force.

That afternoon I took the bus to naval headquarters. Perhaps they would have additional information, or possibly something could be done to change the orders. I approached the chief clerk in the personnel office. He was a dour old chap, his heavy jowls giving him the appearance of a dyspeptic bulldog. I had barely told him what my orders were when he shoved back his chair, rose ponderously to his feet, and extended a ham-shaped hand. Without expression in his voice he said, "Good luck, sir . . . and good-by, sir." "What do you mean?"

"Well, sir, you've been ordered to an attack transport. That's the newest thing out. They're going to use those ships to carry the troops right up to the beaches! You can give me a battleship any old day — but not one of those babies."

And so, two weeks later, I left for the West Coast to report for duty aboard Attack Transport Number One.

Reporting for duty aboard a ship is like a lodge ritual; it must be done in a certain way. As I walked down the dock toward the berth of the Doyen, I tried to recall all the things I was supposed to do. "Let's see ... I walk up the gangway and just as I get to the top I salute the quarterdeck. Quarterdeck . . . where is the quarterdeck? Or is it the flag I salute? . . . I guess I'll play it safe; I can see the flag from here. Then I salute the officer of the deck and say, 'Your permission to come aboard, sir?' After that I add, 'Lieutenant Marsden reporting aboard for duty.' Then he's supposed to say, 'Permission granted; glad to have you aboard, sir.' From there on, I guess I'm on my own."

It was easier than I had expected. Either the officer of the deck was equally inexperienced, or else he chose to ignore my feeble salute and mumbled words. At any rate, he was really friendly. Putting out his hand, he greeted me.

"Glad to have you aboard, Marsden. The ship's a mess, but I guess you'll get used to it. Chow's about ready, and if you don't mind waiting a minute till my relief gets here, I'll take you up and show you around."

While I waited for him, I looked over the exterior of the ship. She was a big girl, about five hundred feet in length, with a high superstructure forward and decks built in stair fashion toward the stern. Her two stacks gave her the rakish appearance of a light cruiser. At the moment she did look a mess. My new friend explained why.

"We're not in commission yet. She was due for it a week ago, but something fouled us up, as usual, and we're still waiting. But the Old Man said the big day has been set for May 22, and that's only about a week away."

As the relief O.O.D. approached, my friend unbuckled his gun belt and motioned for me to follow him. It was like walking through a fun house at a carnival. I had no way of knowing where the narrow passageways were leading, and the decks were covered with fire hoses, cables, hissing air hoses, acetylene lines, and helmeted yard workers. After winding through this maze for at least three hundred feet, we took a sharp left turn up a ladder (stairway, I would have called it then). At the top was a small room about twenty feet in length and eleven feet wide. The little sign above the entry labeled it "Ship's Officers' Wardroom."

The ship's officers were already eating when we entered. My friend took me to the head of the table and introduced me to the executive officer. "Commander McClaughry, this is Lieutenant Marsden. He just reported aboard ship for duty with the supply department." Commander McClaughry, a tall, slender, friendly appearing chap, stood up and shook my hand. "Glad to have you with us, Mr. Marsden. We have a good ship here, and I know you'll like it." Other introductions followed. There were so many men to meet that the best I could manage was a grin and a "Glad to meet you."

A few personalities, though, did make a lasting impression. There was Ralph Lane, the chief engineer. He was a huge, heavy-set man with a great booming voice, a man who would say what he liked when he liked. Then there was the senior medical officer, handsome, dapper Jim Oliver, fresh from a society practice in swanky Palm Springs. These two made a place for me at the table, and as the meal continued did their best to acquaint me with the background of the ship and what she was supposed to do.

Although the date was May 17, 1943, the Doyen had been conceived many years before. At the close of World War I it was anticipated that a new type of transport would be needed. Visions of world peace were bright, but the War Department was still skeptical about the security of the small islands in the West Indies group. What was required, the planners reasoned, was a small and speedy transport — a ship just large enough to carry a Marine landing team. Tentative plans were drafted (the rough design was submitted by the youthful Assistant Secretary of the Navy, Franklin Delano Roosevelt) and an estimate was submitted to the Naval Affairs Committee. As the Congress of the early twenties was more interested in scrapping the fleet than in making any additions, the project ended there. A ship of the proposed type was approved, but funds were not made available.

Then came signs of trouble in the East and in the West. From the start of activities in the Pacific, it was evident that a new type of joint land-and-sea warfare had to be developed. "Amphibious" was the only accurate term, and "amphibious warfare" it became. Classical notions and textbook tactics were subjected to a vigorous revaluation in which many were scrapped. Naval and civilian architects spent long hours together over their drafting boards. Plans were turned out only to be discarded as new demands showed them to be inadequate. Ships and boats of weird design slid down the ways. Ponderous floating boxcars, smaller boats with clanking ramps, sleek torpedo boats — all crowded the shipyards and the transportation facilities of the nation. It was then that the original plans for the transport were resurrected.

A fast and maneuverable troopship was required. The Navy Department selected a New York architectural firm, masters in the field of yacht design, to blueprint the working plans. The specifications were rigid; it was to be a vessel more than four hundred feet in length, capable of carrying thirteen hundred men, with storage space for supplies and munitions sufficient for sixty days, and possessing a speed of at least eighteen knots. In addition, provision had to be made for complete antiaircraft armament and for the bulky radio and radar units that are a part of every Navy fighting ship. The keel was laid at the yards of the Consolidated Steel Corporation in Los Angeles, just four months after the blueprints were submitted for approval.

On July 9, 1942, the ship was launched. Named after Brigadier General Charles A. Doyen, United States Marine Corps — who once commanded the Fourth Marine Brigade, which later fought so valiantly at Chateau-Thierry and Belleau Woods — she was christened by his granddaughter, Miss Faye Doyen Johnson.

Although the ship was then in the water, much of the work remained to be done. The finishing of the superstructure, the installation of guns, radio, radar, and the intricate intercommunications system — all typically Navy jobs — had yet to be completed. For this work, the hull was towed into the navy yard at Terminal Island, California, where she now lay.

Almost a week later, on May 22, 1943, the Doyen was accepted for the Navy by Captain S. F. Heim, U.S.N. The commissioning of a naval vessel marks the acceptance of that craft by the Navy Department. It also means that from that day on she is an independent unit of the fleet, entitled to her own commanding officer and to her own commission pennant.

The day was a beautiful one, the kind that Southern California advertises. The warm sun shone down on a ship which was hardly recognizable as the one I had originally boarded. The litter of building had been cleared away. Equipment was neatly stowed, and the whole ship glowed from a fresh coat of deep-blue paint. I was just one of the 475 officers and men who stood smartly at attention on the afterdeck. All of us, I believe, stood just a little straighter, held our heads just a little higher than we ever had before. This was our ship, and we were proud of her.

The actual ceremony was brief. Captain Heim formally signed a few papers and then addressed us: "I need not tell you that your ship is fast and powerful. She has been designed for her mission and is fitted with every modern device to meet and beat the enemy at his own game. I am sure the designers and builders have produced a sturdy body, and that you, the crew, will give that body a living soul and spirit."

As he concluded, the Navy Band assembled on the dock commenced playing "The Star-Spangled Banner." The colors rose slowly toward the top of the mainmast. Just as the ruffle of drums reached its full tempo, a line snarled and the flag momentarily paused. From behind me I heard an indrawn breath and a muttered, "Christ . . . that's bad luck." It was answered by a sharp "Shut up! Look! It's breaking loose." For, almost as if it had been planned as an emphasis to commissioning, the colors snapped up full and free. The U.S.S. Doyen, Attack Transport Number One, had come into being.

Captain Heim then turned the ship over to her first skipper, Commander Paul F. Dugan. Chaplain James J. Doyle concluded the ceremony with the invocation that has been given at the launching of each ship of the United States Navy since 1776, an invocation to which all of us added a silent "Amen."

O Almighty and Eternal God, we invoke Thy Name in blessing upon this Ship, her Captain and Crew, and all those who take passage thereon. Stretch forth Thy right hand over her course, as Thou didst in the tempest on the Sea of Galilee, that she may have safe and tranquil sailings. Guided by the Star of the Sea, may this vessel always reach its haven secure, according to Thy holy will. May the blessing of Almighty God, Father, Son, and Holy Ghost descend upon this ship and all those thereon, and abide there always. Amen.

2. The Adolescent

The Doyen was officially born on May 22, 1943, but like all youngsters, she had to go through a stage of growth and adjustment. Most of her crew were just as inexperienced. Captain Dugan and Commander McClaughry were Naval Academy graduates, but the remainder of us had been recruited largely from civilian life and from the Merchant Marine. It was a case of the rider learning to ride on a horse that had never been ridden.

We were all eager to be under way, to get into the battle, but there was much work to be done first. My own duties began immediately. The boss of the supply department was Lieutenant Commander George E. Schindler. Mr. Schindler — he was a stickler for military etiquette and wouldn't think of allowing us to call him George — was a severe and exacting person. Things had to be just so. He was right, of course, but the rest of us chose to be a little more easygoing. The only times he would relax were during the intervals when we managed to slip away to the officers' club. After a few drinks the boss would get really human, sit down at the piano, and bat out some well-executed jazz. Months later, after I had taken over his job, I realized why he had been so careful. Our assignment was to stock the ship with all its equipment, and it was Schindler's responsibility to make certain that nothing was missing. We really sweated through the first loadings. As all hands were turned out to handle stores, the decks were piled high with food, rain gear, nuts and bolts, and just about every other item ever listed in a mail-order catalogue.

This work, though, served to unify the ship's personnel. After one week, I remember writing home that this ship was the friendliest place I had ever known. Everyone was willing to cooperate, for we all realized that someday our own lives might hang in the balance if real teamwork wasn't achieved.

All the troubles weren't concerned with the ordinary work routines of the Doyen. A ship in port within the continental limits of the United States is always faced with some disciplinary problems. In wartime that factor is increased. Members of the crew who had been at sea fell into two classes: those who respected the rules governing liberty in order to protect their rights to further freedom, and those who preferred to disappear from the ship to return just before sailing time. The influence of both groups was felt by our newly assigned recruits.

One mess attendant, a double for Stepin Fechit, hit the beach and the bottle to such an extent that he became involved in what he termed "a little affair with straightedge razors." Another youngster, Red O'Neil from Oklahoma, went on a weekend party with only a twenty-four-hour pass. He was brought back to the ship by the shore patrol and was restricted as prisoner-at-large. Apparently he had made further plans, for one night he slipped over the side, down a cargo net, and on into town. The next morning he appeared before the officer of the deck, saluted smartly, and reported: "Seaman O'Neil, PAL, AWOL, sir."

We had one setback in our work. Shortly before the Doyen was commissioned, we had heard rumors that she was top-heavy. Her hull lines were those of a yacht, yet she possessed a huge superstructure. The grapevine scuttlebutt reported the yard was laying bets two to one that the ship would turn over when she hit the heavy swells off San Francisco. The story was given added impact when, during our second week as an accepted ship of the Navy, we were ordered into dry dock for an inclination test. All of us, from the men in the bilges to the commanding officer, were keeping our collective fingers crossed.

We were bitterly disappointed to learn that in order to make an inclination test the ship had to be stripped of all her supplies, the same supplies we had just so laboriously loaded. But the job had to be done. Then the ship was put in dry dock, and a small flatcar loaded with weights was placed on a railroad track affair which had been laid across the deck amidships. A plumb bob was suspended from a girder of the dry dock. As the flatcar was shifted from one side to the other, a trained technician measured the degree of inclination as shown by the vertical bob. From these figures the ship's seaworthiness in rough weather could be accurately determined.

While the Doyen was being tested, only one representative of the ship was allowed to stay aboard. The rest of us lined the sides of the dry dock and anxiously waited. Commander McClaughry remained on the ship, stationed at a point in its exact center. Ralph Lane chided him, "Commander, you must have a helluva lot of pull around here. What's the story, do you know a congressman?"

"No, sir!" came the quick reply. "They chose me because I part my hair in the middle."

Rumors to the contrary, the ship came through with an excellent record. We were told that she could withstand any sea, and with that report came orders to get under way within forty-eight hours for a brief training cruise. Back came the supplies. But this time we didn't have a week in which to load them. Boxes and crates were piled everywhere. Schindler paced the deck like a madman. "God," he muttered again and again, "how'll we ever know where any thing's stowed? There'll be ramifications; I know there'll be ramifications."

On schedule, two days later, we slid through the breakwater and headed for the open sea. It was after dark when we reached deep water. Though the report had told us that the ship could take anything, most of us were more than dubious. Swaddled in life jackets, a half dozen of us congregated in the officers' wardroom to spend the night. Ensign Dan Minnich, a tall good-natured chap, veteran of the Murmansk run, did his best to increase our uneasiness. Over and over again he declared that the "metacentric center was too high" and "When she tips, you fellows'll see." Bosun Trippler, an old-time Navy man, was inclined to agree with him. After four hours of uneventful cruising, without so much as a 10-degree roll, three of us trooped off to bed. But Dan and Trippler remained where they were sitting. The last thing I heard as I left was Dan saying, "Tripp, I'll bet I beat you to the weather deck when she tips."

The Doyen's initiation was not without real excitement. During our trial run just outside San Diego, all of us were at our battle stations for gunfire practice. Firing was fast, noisy, and continuous, but not too accurate. Almost at the close of the drill, two of the three-inch-fifties got overheated and jammed with live shells still in their partially opened breeches. The condition was immediately reported to the bridge, and the order to cease firing was given.

I watched what happened next. Chief Gunner's Mate Capo and Gunner's Mate "Ace" Parker gingerly approached the guns. While one pulled back on the breech mechanism, the other tugged at the shell. The first came out easily and Capo tossed it overboard. The second, however, was firmly lodged. Grabbing up a small crowbar, Capo slid the point behind the rim of the shell and began to pry it out. This was really dangerous; should the shell be exploded by the heat of the gun, the two men wouldn't have a chance. But the shell finally worked loose into the hands of Ace Parker. We were standing so silently that we could all hear the plop as the shell dropped into the sea. That afternoon at Captain's Mast both men were awarded Letters of Commendation. This was Capo's second decoration; he already held the Silver Star for heroism on the cruiser Northampton.

During that same run the damage control officer conducted a test of the fire-fighting apparatus of the ship. Because of a mechanical defect in the control system, a carbon dioxide extinguisher was mistakenly set off in the after engine room. The engineers on boiler watch in the lower level of the room, unaware of the accumulation of the gas, continued working until they were overcome.

When the engine room failed to respond to a signal from the bridge, the trouble was detected. There wasn't time to outfit a rescue party with oxygen masks. Three engineers on the upper level of the engine room volunteered to attempt to bring out their unconscious shipmates. They crawled down the ladder, fighting for breath at each step, and managed to locate the victims. With the men hung limply over their shoulders, the three engineers worked their way back up to the top of the ladder. Oden V. Hayes, C. L. Greenwood, and J. T. Strauss were later given the Navy and Marine Corps Medal.

By the middle of July the ship was beginning to possess a definite "soul and spirit." Like the intricate engine-room parts, we, her crew, were at last becoming broken in to smooth teamwork. Morale was high and all of us were waiting for the day when we would at last see real action. We felt that time was not very far distant. Even the bootblack boys in San Diego knew that the complete retaking of the Aleutians was about to commence. It was no surprise, then, when the official announcement came: "All departments make ready for sea."

3. Invasion in Dress Blues

Combat loaded, we sailed from San Francisco on July 29. This was our first invasion trip. For most of us, it was the moment when the war became real. This departure was different from the few we had experienced on our brief training cruises. This time we might not be returning.

Tom Hawk, the young officer who had greeted me when I first came aboard, stood with me near the stern rail. It is hard to describe our feelings, feelings shared at that moment by the other crew and troop members who, like us, were lining the rails of the weather decks. As we passed under the Golden Gate Bridge, I remember wondering just how long it would be before I would see it again. Words of a little jingle kept going through my mind. "The Golden Gate in Forty-Eight; The Golden Gate in Forty-Eight." I thought, too, of my wife, whom I had left twenty-four hours before in our hotel room. Though the San Francisco skyline was misty with haze, I tried to pick out the hotel building. It seemed odd that in all that huge city there was only one person, one tiny person, who cared that I was leaving.

The blaring horns of harbor craft snapped me out of my reverie. We weren't leaving forever; we were part of the United States Navy and we'd be coming back.

Though our destination had not yet been revealed, the ski-troopers aboard and our large store of winter clothing left little to be guessed. Just four months before, in a bitterly contested battle, U.S. troops had succeeded in wresting Attu and Adak islands from the Japs — the first step in recovering the Aleutians. It was only reasonable to assume that this invasion was to be the follow-through. The Army rations, something new at that time, were labeled K, and our ignorance prompted us to believe that the K was a destination address. The shipboard "authorities" were unanimous in naming Kiska as our goal. Our second day out this was officially confirmed.

We were all new at the game — amphibious operations were still in their infancy — and perhaps our inexperience added spice to what might otherwise have been a routine voyage. As the Doyen approached the Arctic Circle we could almost see the increase in tension. Happy-go-lucky boys of two weeks ago were now thin-lipped men. It was no longer necessary to tell the lookouts to keep on the alert; almost every wave, and certainly every porpoise, was sighted and accounted for.

After five days of steady steaming, our task group was well into enemy waters. The pleasant weather of the California coast had given way to days and nights of intermittent fog. Extra bridge watches were posted; we worked and slept in our life jackets. We had no doubt that this was the real thing.

The day of August 2 progressed smoothly enough. True, a few reports of contacts with enemy submarines were submitted by our destroyer screen, but no subs were actually sighted. With nightfall a sense of security began to pervade the ship. The wardroom was checkered with little groups of troop and ship's company officers. A few card games were in progress. Down in the troop mess hall, members of a Negro loading battalion had met for a combination community sing and revival meeting.

At 2130 the comparative quiet of the ship was shattered by the clanging of the general alarm. Thrown into a 45-degree turn, the ship listed heavily to the starboard; loose gear went skidding across the decks. The effect of the intensive training of the past weeks was apparent; battle stations were manned almost instantly. Rumors spread throughout the ship: We were under torpedo attack . . . the ship ahead of us had been torpedoed . . . the task unit ahead of us had made contact with the enemy fleet. The colored troops in the mess hall were probably the most affected. They had no battle stations; they had to wait and listen. As they were giving way to fear and confusion, the colored chaplain intervened. Jumping on top of a table, he shouted to his group: "Men! Men! I've just been talking to the Lord . . . and He's on our side!" The effect in calming the panic was miraculous.

A few minutes later over the public-address system came the welcome news that the submarine contact had proved to be false.

Fully clothed, I rolled into my bunk and tried to get some sleep. Again and again, just as I began to doze off, someone would run across the deck above my stateroom. Or I would hear the distant thud of depth charges. Sleep would not come.

All of us remained overalert. At least a dozen torpedo wakes were reported by the lookouts. Had it not been for the efficient coverage provided by our destroyer screen, morale might well have been generally disrupted. But each report we submitted was checked, and in each case was shown to have been the result of someone's imagination.

On the afternoon of August 3, again in the midst of soupy fog, the stern lookout excitedly reported to the bridge: "A floating object is approaching from the stern!" The officer of the deck immediately notified the commanding officer.

"What does it look like?" Captain Dugan demanded.

"Sir, it looks like a Jap PT boat!"

The captain and the "exec" hurried to the afterdeck. There, looming through the mist, was the U.S.S. Thuban, an attack-cargo vessel of our own group. The squadron had made a zigzag turn; the Thuban, which had been alongside, had swung in on our stern. The lookout, not realizing this, had been understandably confused. But it was a long time before his shipmates allowed him to forget about the incident.

On August 5 our task group pulled into Kukla Bay at Adak, Alaska. Since recovery of the base in April, it had undergone a great change. It was now a fully equipped and humming naval supply depot. In the week that followed, stores were replenished and more troops were embarked. This period was marked by one tragic accident.

During loading operations one of the landing craft was swung next to the rail to facilitate the work. A young sailor, Joe Bata, seaman first class, reached over to place a fender between the boat and the ship's side. At that moment a huge ground swell rolled the ship. Frantically Joe attempted to step back. He was just a little too late. The swinging boat banged against the Doyen and cleanly nipped off the youngster's right arm. For him the war was over.

On August 14 we sailed for Kiska. This was the pay run. The battlewagons of the fleet had gone on ahead some days before and were already pounding the beaches of Kiska with heavy artillery.

Excitement ran high and nerves were on edge. But that night we were given something to gripe about, something to help take our minds off the coming battle. The weather had been cold, and all of us, officers and men alike, had kept warm by wearing any kind of clothing we could find. Although Captain Dugan was unusually strict where clothing regulations were concerned, he realized that we did have to stay warm. But his good humor ended when Ensign Dan Minnich reported to the bridge clad in a bright-checkered smoking jacket.

"Take that damn thing off and get below!" the Old Man thundered. "And," he shouted to the O.O.D., "pass the word for all hands to put on dress blues." And so, on the eve of the invasion of Kiska, the personnel of the Doyen paused in their work to get dressed up.

In direct contrast to our attitude was the mood of the combat troops we were carrying. The group we had picked up at Adak were the toughest bunch of fighters we had ever seen. Called the Rangers, they had spent almost a year in the Arctic zone getting hardened up for cold-weather fighting. Most of them had hated the duty and, by the time we picked them up, had reached the point where they hated just about everything and everybody. They were a bloodthirsty bunch and were obviously eager to get ashore. At 2130, although H-hour was still a long way off, they were already combat packed and standing in line in the blacked-out passageways.

At 0130 on August 15 Kiska Island was sighted. We anchored approximately three miles off the coast at a point near Quisling Cove. Through the half-light of the Arctic morning we could see the rugged coast line. Towering almost in front of us was a huge perpendicular cliff fronted by a shallow beach. It was on this beach that the troops were scheduled to land.

At 0620 the first wave of troops headed for the land. As the men left our ship, they were like a group of football players heading for the field; their raw animal optimism was almost contagious.

I climbed the ladder to the radio shack, thinking that we might be able to pick up the progress as it was reported from the beach. A release beamed to the command vessel was just coming in. "Patrol party reports finding hot coffee in Jap trench . . . requests directions . . . over." We were unable to pick up the reply, but a few minutes later we could hear the boom of mortar fire. It was obvious that a patrol had been sent forward to investigate. Soon the radio burst out again. "Patrol reports coffee left by party of Rangers . . . sorry . . . out."

The word that the Japs had apparently evacuated the island came shortly afterward. Because such a report could not be verified until a complete survey of the island had been made, landing operations continued as planned. Mountains of supplies and equipment were ferried into the cove. Since the beach at that point was extremely narrow — not more than a hundred yards wide — it wasn't long before the crates and boxes had formed a massive pile forty feet deep. To aid in handling the traffic, the beach party of the Doyen was sent ashore. Lew Sayers, the beachmaster, and Al Kelly, beach-party surgeon, led the group.

After Doc Kelly returned to the ship, we cornered him for his impressions of the fight on the beach. Doc was a bit tired, but after a warm shower and a tremendous meal of spaghetti, he let us follow him up to his room. He seated himself on his bed and the rest of us took over the chairs, desks, and wastebaskets. In a quiet sort of a voice, Doc began.

"Well, the first troops didn't meet any opposition. But the going was tough, darn tough. That tundra was a mucky slime almost a foot deep — even on the sides of the cliff. During the daylight, reconnaissance units were sent on ahead and the bulk of the men stayed behind to help us organize beach defense and supply. This beach defense outfit was pretty fouled up ... I don't mean that they didn't know their job, but they were a trigger-happy bunch. Jeez! The only men killed were the ones they potted. Their own men, mind you . . . those who went out in the advance groups."

"How come, Doc?" someone asked. "Didn't they have any signals worked out?"

"Sure, they had 'em worked out all right. A fellow was telling me the Army linguists had told them no Jap could pronounce words filled with the letter l — that is, pronounce them like an American. So they had two passwords, lollypop and pollylop. They had countersigns, too, like a raised right arm. But what the experts didn't figure on was that damn fog and its effect on those nerve-tensed soldiers."

Doc worked his way under the covers. It was obvious that he was getting sleepy, but we had to hear the rest of it. "Did you see any Japs, Doc?"

"Nary a one. The nearest thing we saw to a Nip was one of their dogs, and he was a mongrel at that. But we did see some of their booby traps. One fellow was plowing through the tundra — not even on a path — when one of the things exploded and bowled him into the air like a tenpin. Another soldier picked up a sewing basket . . . Why'd he be crazy enough to do that? Imagine not knowing that a sewing basket would be a trap! Well, anyhow, he picked the thing up and it started sizzling. He heaved it back on the ground and started to run. Then he must've realized that a lot of us standing around there would be killed if he didn't do something. So he turned around, went back to the basket, and stood on it. The charge must have been small or something. It went off with quite a bang, but it didn't even budge him. He was really one surprised boy."

"What took you so long getting back?" I asked. Doc looked even more sleepy, but he had evidently decided there was no getting rid of us.

"Do you remember seeing that picture of a Negro in a wrecked boat way out in the middle of the ocean? You know the one ... the picture with all the sharks swimming around the boat? Well, I know just how he felt. We got the order to return to the ship at 1645. Fog had set in and visibility was absolutely zero. But orders were orders. Lew and I ordered the gang into the boat and we shoved off. And that water was plenty rough, I'm telling you. After about five minutes of pitching and tossing, there wasn't one of us that had the slightest idea where we were. We couldn't see a darn thing, not even the outline of a ship. Lew had a pretty good idea, though; he stopped the boat every now and then and waited to hear the fog horns of any near-by ships. That's the way we located the Doyen. If it hadn't been for that nasal fog horn of ours, we'd probably be fifty miles out to sea by now.

"But getting back to the ship was just half the battle. By the time we reached the ship, the waves were so high we couldn't come alongside the gangway. They had to lower two Jacob's ladders for us. Boy, what a job it was to get on them! Our first mooring line parted, and we barely managed to make the second line fast. Then we fastened life lines around ourselves, and each of us made a jump for the ladders. I almost had to be hauled aboard; I jumped for the first ladder and missed it. Just at that moment, though, the Doyen rolled and practically tossed the second ladder right in my face."

Kelly decided that his story was completed. Rather than argue with us, he reached up and flicked out his light.

On August 18 we rounded the island to Vega Harbor, where a few ambulatory casualties were brought aboard. The most common complaint was that of cold feet — "foot immersion," the doctors called it. From Vega Harbor we proceeded to Adak to discharge the remainder of our troops and cargo.

Our first operation was over and the biggest thing that had happened to us was the order to go into combat in dress blues. I suppose we should have felt happy about it; actually, most of us felt rather let down. We were glad when we received our next orders.

In the company of the strangest convoy ever provided a lone transport, we nosed out of Kukla Bay and headed southward for the Hawaiian Islands. The screen consisted of a battleship, a heavy cruiser, and two destroyers. The Doyen — veteran of the great invasion of Kiska — was indeed a proud ship.

4. Pollywog versus Shellback

Neptunus Rex, Ruler of the Raging Main, extends greetings to Captain Dugan and to all the loyal Shellback subjects aboard the good ship Doyen. To the many lowly Pollywogs, he issues solemn warning. By virtue of Royal Decree, he commands that all said Pollywogs be duly initiated into the mysteries of the deep on the fifteenth day of October, nineteen hundred and forty-three.

/s/ Davy Jones

His Majesty's Scribe

This message, received via seaweed cablegram, came as we headed from Pearl Harbor, where we had refueled and provisioned, southward toward New Zealand. Those of us who had never crossed the equator — the majority of the officers and crew — were naturally dubious about the forthcoming activities. Such proceedings smacked of childishness, even of sadism. But that was the attitude of the pollywogs. Among the few shellbacks the situation was different. Clandestine meetings began to take place. In the C.P.O. quarters, the wardroom, the sail locker, and in some of the smaller living compartments, men gathered in little whispering groups. Usually the meetings were marked by occasional outbursts of uncontrolled laughter. The supply storeroom was robbed of its stocks of red, yellow, and green cloth. Pieces of canvas were hurriedly shaped into hard-packed billies. Now and then we had glimpses of dress rehearsals, of gaily clad pirates, buxom-bosomed girls, somber undertakers.

We pollywogs had one occasion to do a little plotting of our own. The announcement had been made that a court of three trusted shellbacks would check the credentials of each officer and man who claimed to have previously crossed the equator. The only acceptable evidence was to be a signed and sealed Davy Jones certificate. One of the doctors, an easygoing, heavy-set boy named Jaskunas, had a very definite opinion of such technicalities. During a bull session in Doc Oliver's room, he blurted out in a grudging voice, "That system isn't at all fair . . . there's no way to get around it! Or is there?"

Jas was a great idea man, who liked nothing better than a good practical joke. He found a blank certificate and with painstaking care filled it in.

According to the almost illegible handwriting, he had crossed the line in 1934, enroute to Sydney, Australia, on a combination freighter and passenger liner, the James S. Bullsby. With the bribed assistance of the chief yeoman in the ship's office, he had the ship's seal placed on the document. The expert use of a stylus made the impression almost indiscernible. To give the certificate the proper amount of aging, he rubbed it on the deck and then folded and refolded it. We had to agree that it looked genuine.

When Jas was called before the judges, he calmly handed the certificate to the chairman. That worthy gentleman, weather-beaten Chief Master-at-Arms Slattery, scanned it once and pronounced, "Looks o.k. to me. What do the rest of you think?" Warrant Officer Timmins, a shrewd Irishman who placed little faith in the claims of anyone he had not seen cross the line, took it upon himself to ask some questions.

"You crossed the line in 1934 . . . that's a long time ago. What were you doing on the ship?" Jas replied without hesitation.

"Mother and I were on a summer cruise; I was just a kid then." Jas was on his dignity now and had almost convinced himself that he was actually a shellback. "I'm telling you gentlemen that I crossed the line. Isn't my word good enough for you?"

"All right, all right." Timmins pretended to pacify him. "We don't really doubt you; this is only a formality. Just one more question. You say you went to Sydney . . . what was the first thing you saw when you entered Sydney Harbor?"

Jas was nonplussed. The question was a trap, and he didn't know what to answer. But he gamely hazarded, "A long breakwater."

"Wrong!" Timmins jumped to his feet. "This miserable pollywog is a liar. There's no breakwater at Sydney. The harbor is formed by a bunch of low mountains!"

When Jas returned to Oliver's room, where the rest of us were waiting, he was smoldering with genuine rage. "That bunch of pirates wouldn't take my word for it," he growled.

On the morning of the fourteenth the ship's activities were stopped by the call for all pollywogs to muster on the upper deck aft. A few minutes later the boom of a drum was heard, and over its steady thumping came the piercing squeal of a bosun's pipe. We stood nervously at attention, not knowing quite what to expect.

Down the starboard passageway came the sound of shuffling feet. The rolling of drums grew louder. Then from around the corner came the most bloodcurdling procession of assorted cutthroats seen since the days of Captain Kidd. In the lead swaggered a huge, six-foot pirate. Complete from earrings to wide-topped boots, he strode up and down the lines of pollywogs, whacking first one and then another of us into resentful attention. Behind him followed a small group of similarly dressed ruffians — each wearing a large badge designating him as an official policeman.

The "Royal Guard" formed a semicircle facing us. In a froggish voice the lead pirate commanded, "Kneel, you slimy pollywogs, kneel!" The menace of the swinging clubs was convincing. We knelt. "O most mighty Davy Jones," the speaker continued, "the scum are ready." Into the half circle stumped another pirate. In one hand he carried a trident, the forked symbol of his royal master, and in the other, a tightly rolled scroll. The drumming ceased.

"Mac McHaffie," Davy Jones intoned, "step forward and hear the charges placed against you." Lieutenant McHaffie, Marine troop quartermaster, stepped forward. "You are charged with the dismal crime of being a Marine. A Horse Marine without a horse. The court will hear your defense tomorrow morning. That is all." Moving his finger down the list, Jones came to another name. "Clifford Hanlin, storekeeper second class, approach and hear your indictment. It is reported that you believe all shellbacks are sea-lawyers and sissies, that you said the royal queen was a two-bit tramp. Your defense will be difficult . . . very difficult."

One after another, we stepped before the royal scribe. The list of offenses was long. Finally, after the last man had been subpoenaed, Davy Jones announced: "Neptunus Rex and his royal family will board your ship tomorrow morning at nine o'clock. The royal court will assemble, and at that time your cases will be judged. Until then, I leave you all to the mercy of the trusty shellbacks now present." The drum beats commenced again, and single file, Davy Jones and his retinue disappeared down the passageway.

The "trusty shellbacks" needed no encouragement. That afternoon was marked by many skirmishes, in which the ship's officers received their share of attention. Deciding to be discreet, I went up to my room. But not for long. Two of the policemen rapped on my door and invited me to come with them. "It won't be bad," one of them confidentially assured me. "We just want you to scrub a few bunk bottoms."

Had I known what was actually in store, I would have pulled on a few extra pairs of trousers. We filed through the passageway, down the ladder, and out onto the foc'sle deck.

Bam! Scarcely had I stepped into the open when I was caught up and thrown heavily to the deck. It was wet and slippery, and I slithered across it for a good five feet. "Get in there and work!" someone shouted, accenting his words with a terrific wallop from a billie. It caught me across the back, and I jerked up onto my knees. "Make way for a new scum," the voice continued. The maze of legs in front of me parted, and I was able to see some of the other pollywogs. Surrounded by a circle of arms and clubs, they were groveling on their hands and knees, scrubbing canvas bunk bottoms. A fire hose had been hitched up and the terrific force of the salt water was brought to bear first on one and then on another. A well-placed kick sent me among them. Someone handed me a brush and a bar of soap. Automatically I started to scrub.

"Faster," another tormentor howled, and he walloped me across the rump with a club that must have been filled with cement. It hurt. I worked furiously. "He's slow; he can work faster than that. Give him some more!" At least three clubs hit me. They weren't tender blows, or just the stinging type. It was an honest-to-God clubbing.

I was glad I was soaked with water; tears of hurt and anger poured down my cheeks. I was mad clear through, and there was nothing I could do about it. I knew what it was to want to kill. Over and over under my breath I muttered, "You dirty bunch of —— you bunch of ——." I noticed that a few of the fellows who had got there earlier were sitting on the deck as much as they possibly could. I followed their example.

Just as I was beginning to think I had learned the combination, someone jerked me by the collar and ordered me to scrub Mac McHaffie's back. I began. "Harder!" yelled my tormentor. He bashed me across the small of my back so hard I almost jumped at him. Mac's back must have been made of tough stuff; at least it was scrubbed as it never had been before.

After what seemed hours of torture, I was told to get to my feet. It was hard to stand up. My rump no longer had any feeling. It was so swollen that my pants were drawn skin tight. "Follow me," someone ordered. "You're going to have the privilege of testing the barber chair." Back we filed across the deck, up the ladder, down a passageway, and on to the fantail of the ship.

Mac McHaffie was there ahead of me. Mac, a football coach in civilian life, was the type of chap who would rather be beaten into insensibility than show any signs of physical pain. He was told to remove his shoes and sit down in the chair. When the electric contact was thrown, I could see Mac's muscles quiver. But he didn't even open his mouth. After five minutes of the treatment, the shellbacks grudgingly let him go. I was next, and I wasn't made of such stern stuff. The first jolt of electric juice hit me like a thousand needles, and I leaped a foot out of the chair. I was thrown back into it. "What are you?" a tough-looking sailor barked.

"Pollywog," I managed to blurt out.

"Say it so they can hear you up forward," he commanded. Another spurt of electricity was a good prompter.

"I'm a slimy pollywog!" I screamed. They were satisfied, and I managed to limp out of the chair.

Much later that night I lay on my stomach in the upper bunk. Doc Oliver had administered ointment plus an unexpected toddy of brandy and pineapple juice. Tom Hawk came into the room, pulled down his pants, and with great pride showed me his memento of the day. It was a livid welt almost an inch high. Doc Oliver, just across the way, heard him. "You haven't seen anything," he called out. "Just take a look at Larry's rump. It'll be at least three months before it heals up."

When I finally dozed off, it was to dream of the fiendish tortures I wanted to inflict on my shellback shipmates. I knew that all this was just part of an ancient game, but it did seem to me that it had been carried too far.

Early on the morning of the fifteenth lookouts were posted to watch for the equator. Sweltering under layers of woolen underwear, wool socks, winter jackets, and stocking caps, eighteen men paced stolidly back and forth on the weather decks. The first lieutenant, Stan Gay, was the pollywog officer-in-charge. His outfit was the most burdensome of all. It was a full-length, air-tight, asbestos fire-fighting suit. With its helmet it much resembled a deep-sea diving outfit. He claimed afterward he had felt like a fish being boiled in its own oil. The senior watch officer, an extremely serious chap who had been a Philadelphia attorney, had the task of leveling the ocean. With a bucket attached to a fifty-foot line, he laboriously hoisted a gallon of water from the port side of the ship and carried it across the captain's quarterdeck, only to dump it back into the sea on the starboard side. It might have been amusing for the first twenty trips.

The official initiation began at ten o'clock. With the same elaborate pomp that had marked the arrival of Davy Jones, Neptunus Rex and his court came aboard. The royal queen and the princesses were scarcely recognizable as former shipmates. With more exaggeration than accuracy, burlap brassieres covered breasts that would have done credit to the lady on the pink Police Gazette. Grass skirts revealed long, knobby legs, and here and there a pair of pink panties. (Where they came from, no one could ever guess.) The royal baby, chosen for his rotund shape, was Bosun's Mate "Irish" Bowdren. Encased in a grease-stained diaper, he settled himself in a specially constructed high chair and proceeded to play pitty-pat against his huge, furry stomach. Before this grotesque assembly we pollywogs were herded.

The royal court was in session at the top of the ladder leading from the boat deck to the upper deck aft. A chute had been placed on the rungs, and at the bottom, in two eager lines, waited at least fifteen bloodthirsty shellbacks.

Doc Gilfillan, our dignified family doctor from Iowa, was first in line. As he approached the bench of justice, presided over by an owlish-looking inquisitor, he was helped along by the sting of an electrically charged spear.

"You are accused of being a lieutenant commander without ever having crossed the line. Do you plead guilty or not guilty?" Doc tried to be brave. Though jigging from the effects of the electricity, he gasped out, "Not guilty." The judge turned to the defense attorney, a young Chinese American noted for his misuse of the English language. "What do you say?" roared the judge. The Chinese boy grinned from behind an enormous pair of horn-rimmed glasses. "Doctor, he velly nice man . . . but he guilty as hell!" The gavel banged and Doc Gil went hurtling down the chute.

One by one we followed him in rapid order. As we hit the bottom of the slide, we were hammered through the double line until we reached the chair of the royal dentist. There we were jerked into a sitting position, our mouths were pried open, and a solution resembling kerosene and turpentine was administered. It was only one step and two whacks to the operating table of the royal surgeon. Stripped to the waist, we were blindfolded, slapped down on the hard table, and prodded and jabbed with bread-kneading industry. Operations were performed with a huge chunk of ice.

We were then ushered in the usual manner to the tunnel of love. Constructed from a fifty-foot wind sail, the canvas tube measured not more than two feet in diameter. Into the front gushed a forced stream of sea water, and along the entire length stood watchful shellbacks, batting away at any visible bulge, unconcerned about what that bulge might represent.

Some of us tried to rush through the tunnel on all fours. That was a mistake. More observant followers chose to snake through on their stomachs. Though almost drowned by the cascading water, they were at least spared the bludgeons. Emerging like newborn pups, we were again helped along to the next station, the royal barber.

The barber chair, my old friend of the day before, was mounted on the edge of a seven-foot tank. I had a glimpse of its contents, a watery mess of grease and garbage.

The haircutter had apparently been schooled in the jungle. His work would have warranted the praise of a Malayan head-hunter. Lotion was lavishly applied from the end of a graphite gun, and bystanders aided by applying egg shampoos.

"Want to get out?" the barber asked. Without waiting for an answer, his helpers shoved the chair backwards, catapulting me head first into the slush below. I came up gasping and sputtering.

"What are you?" howled the attendants.

"Pollywog!" I replied. Down I went again. "Shellback" was the proper answer. I learned rapidly.

"All right, shellback — get the hell out of there!" As I scrambled up the net suspended along one side, my attackers took their last swings at me.

I was met by the royal chaplain. "Kiss the book!" he demanded. Ready to agree to anything, I plunged my face between the leaves of the proffered volume — leaves lined with dirty bacon rind.

That was all. A few of the hardy ones stood around to watch their friends come through. The rest of us were content to stagger up to our bunks, glad that this day happened but once in a lifetime. Maybe this was an ancient type of sport, but it should have died with the Dark Ages.

5. Those New Zealand Women

"Boy oh boy! Women! Millions of 'em!" That was the story of the men as they stumbled up the gangway after the first day of liberty in Wellington, New Zealand. Almost a month of steady steaming had made them appreciative. I was downright envious as I watched them troop aboard; I had been on duty all that day in the stuffy confines of the supply office.

Early the next morning, in the company of Keith Petty, our disbursing officer, and Tom Hawk, I left the ship. It was just a short walk from the waterfront to the business district of the city. My first impression was that I had walked into a Hollywood setting of San Francisco in the early 1900's. Rickety trolley cars clanked down the hilly streets. Vintage cars, many of them Fords, chugged patiently along the left sides of the thoroughfares. Bicycles seemed to be everywhere. Men and women stopped in little groups along the way, some to exchange gossip, some for a spot of tea. Life seemed to be slow-moving and pleasant. Even the styles were not of today. Men wore tweed knickers and visor caps; women dressed in modest, long-skirted styles.

After wandering about for hours in a sort of sentimental daze, we climbed aboard one of the trolleys and headed out toward the residential district. The car was crowded and we began the trip standing up. Before we had gone more than a block, though, a group of women on one of the long side seats bunched together and motioned us to sit down next to them. We did, with alacrity:

In most cities we would have gone on in silence. But not in Wellington. One of our benefactors, a tall, rawboned girl, smiled at us and asked, "How do you like our country?" It wasn't an original question, but it served to start the conversation. We gave the expected answer that it was pretty wonderful. "But not so nice as your United States, is it?"

I started to make a gallant reply, but Tom, in his usual impulsive fashion, blurted out, "I'll say it isn't! You girls should see Indianapolis. Boy! That's really the town!" Tom didn't stop there; he began a one-man dissertation on all forty-eight states, and did an effective job of gaining all the girls' interest. This was discouraging, so Keith and I turned back to our original project of sightseeing.

We were passing through the old section of the city. The houses here were stiff and imposing, trimmed with fancy work and cupolas. Lawns, when they existed, were small. A little farther on we entered the suburban area. Here there were houses of the most modern design. Just as I was getting interested in a weird modernistic creation along the way, I heard one of the girls exclaim, "Oh! You Americans. Here you've made us miss our stop!" Then she said to Tom in a low warm voice, "But I don't really mind . . . you're such an interesting man."

Tom had but one comment. "I don't think I've ever seen a more friendly country."

Noontime came, and with it a desire for food. We were downtown again, and we wandered along looking for a good place to eat. We passed one hotel, the principal one in Wellington, and looked through the windows into the dining room. It was comparable to the finest in the United States. There were, however, more pieces of silverware. Keith and I were willing to try it, but Tom insisted that we find some more interesting place, some spot, as he put it, with more "color."

A few steps down the walk brought us to a milk bar. It was modernistic in design, with a huge glass-block entryway. Inside it sparkled with white porcelain. But again Tom had the same objection. We went on. Turning up one of the side streets, we came to what must have been the cheaper restaurant district. Even though the air was brisk, we could smell the odors of cooking. One cafe had its menu posted on the window. "Steak and eggs, $.30." It was irresistible.

The cafe was a dump of a place, dingy and badly lighted. The tea-sized tables were covered with stained oilcloth and there was no array of silverware. Out of the kitchen poured the odor of mutton fat. Keith and I were ready to leave, but this place seemed to please Tom. "What was it you wanted," Keith queried, "color or odor?" But the steaks were good, and the milk and butter even better.

That afternoon we took a cab out to the country club. Golf, always the Englishman's favorite, was popular in Wellington. Clubs and balls had been donated by members for the use of servicemen, and we spent a pleasant four hours dubbing around the course. It was hilly country and we finally stopped after fourteen holes. We must have had a weary limp as we headed from the club house, for a car just pulling out of the drive came to a halt and a woman put her head through the window and called, "Would you like a lift?" We climbed into the back seat of the car.

The lady, a comely blond of about forty, turned around in the seat and introduced herself. "I'm Mrs. Muir, and this is my husband, Doctor Muir." We told them about the Doyen and where we had already been. It seemed almost no time before we were in the heart of town. Doctor Muir, for the first time taking his attention from the driving, asked us to stop in at their house for a few drinks.

The New Zealand beer had a mellowing influence, and as we gathered about the fireplace, the doctor entertained us with stories of his local practice. The invasion of Americans had greatly affected New Zealand. In his pleasantly precise voice, he told us of the many illegitimate children he had delivered in the past year. "Personally," he concluded, "I think it has been a fine thing. We're a small country ... inclined to inbreed. We need some new blood down here."

Mrs. Muir added that most of the girls preferred American men to those of their own country. "It's because they treat women so well," she explained, smiling apologetically at her husband.

When dinner time came — about eight o'clock — our host insisted that we stay. A new arrival, his attractive young niece, provided an added inducement.

After dinner Doctor Muir drove us down to the dock. As we were saying good night, he added that his niece would be very happy to entertain us during the remainder of our stay. "My wife," he continued, "also enjoys dancing, but I'm afraid I'm a little too old for it. I should have no objections if one of you would care to escort her for an evening." His tone was completely sincere.

Many of the other officers and men had similar experiences. A passenger officer aboard our ship met a pretty little blonde at the race tracks. After spending the afternoon with her, he suggested an evening date. She was completely agreeable. At the end of a spirited night of dining, drinking, and dancing, he finally escorted her to her home. As is the custom among Marines, he suggested that she invite him into the house. They entered the living room. There, seated in an easy chair, was a young New Zealander. As he rose to be introduced, the young lady said to her escort, "This is my husband." Like a tardy boy confronted by a truant officer, the American began to look for the door. It was some minutes before he could fully appreciate the first words of the young husband, "You folks would probably like to be alone. If you will excuse me, I'll go up to bed."

Whatever the cause of this lend-lease spirit which most New Zealand men seemed to possess, it was appreciated by the Americans. And so was the equally friendly attitude of the women. The peacetime ratio of women to men had always been high, and the war had increased it. At the race tracks, hotels, and dance halls, groups of unattached women could always be seen. It may have been that the girls had visions of marriage and a migration to the fabulous United States. Or perhaps it was because the girls were naturally friendly and were lonesome for masculine companionship.

Our stay in New Zealand was short and pleasant. We were there just long enough to taste the full spice of the place without longing for some more familiar diet. We spent a share of our time and money at the race tracks. Pari-mutuel betting, in amounts ranging from ten shillings to five pounds, did much to increase the state's financial reserve. A share of our pay checks, too, went for liquor. Off-sale stuff was not to be had except from bootleggers. Since the whiskey in the local bars was a muddy mixture tasting like turpentine, a few of us spent an occasional twenty-five dollars for a quart of Dewar's White Label. Pubs were numerous, but we didn't stay in New Zealand long enough to learn to enjoy the popular mixtures of beer and port wine or beer and gin. Bars or nightclubs as we knew them in the United States could not be found. The nearest substitute was the lounge of the Midland Hotel. But even that had certain disadvantages. Though the highballs served were at least 90 per cent water, the house rules limited sales to residents of the hotel. Doc Oliver claimed that this prohibition was just a subterfuge to increase the tips of the waiters. He handed one of them a few shillings, and the waiter returned in five minutes with a room number.

In the seven days we were in New Zealand many of us established lasting friendships. When the ship was at last combat loaded and ready to sail, there were few among us who were not reluctant to leave. One of the men expressed our attitude by the most sincere tribute a Navy man can pay to a port. As we cleared the harbor heading northward, he was heard to remark, "Gosh, but I'd really like to come back here after the war."

6. Tarawa

Tarawa promised to be an easy invasion. That was the optimistic opinion of the Marine raiders whom we had taken on at Wellington. They felt confident that we would find the Gilbert Islands deserted, that the Japs had planned another Kiska. There was no precise source for that feeling, and the chances are that none existed. It was probably a case of wishful thinking fostered by the impressive sight of our battle forces.

In charge of the operation were Rear Admiral Hill and Major General Holland-Smith. These men, together with their staffs, came aboard the Doyen in New Zealand, intending to use her as a flagship during training maneuvers. It was our first opportunity to watch the high command at work. Admiral Hill was quite brusque. Slender and quick in action, he would pace the quarterdeck rapidly, often worrying aloud over some delay in precalculated action. General Holland-Smith was a decided contrast. Tall and solidly built, he reminded us of a confident and dignified professor of mathematics. When he spoke, it was with precision and studied emphasis.

On the staff was Colonel Edson, the hero of Guadalcanal. From the stories about the reputation of Edson's Raiders that had preceded him, we expected to meet a dashing daredevil sort of man. It was a surprise to learn that the medium-sized, paunchy, balding colonel sitting in the lower wardroom, clad only in shorts and an undershirt, was the man who had reputedly informed his junior officers, "I want to see dead bodies — and I don't care whose they are."

Edson's features are hard to describe. His high, sloping forehead seemed to continue down to the point of his nose. That nose was the focal point of his entire face. His eyes were deep-set, small, and brilliant. His voice was soft. After spending a few minutes with this man, it was easy to understand how he had attained his high degree of personal leadership. He gave the impression of a man who knew his business, who would act fairly and unswervingly, and whose judgment could be trusted.

Amphibious training maneuvers are a combination of basic instruction and dress rehearsal. Though the troops have been trained in the rudiments of ground fighting, the actual procedure of loading and landing has to be practiced. The setting for the maneuvers must be carefully selected so that the sea, the weather, and the terrain closely approximate the conditions of the anticipated invasion point. As far as possible, all movements must be coordinated with the schedules to be used on the pay run.

The island of Efate in the New Hebrides group was chosen by the command for our practice base. Operation plans were studied by each section that would participate. Coordination had to be perfect, and could be achieved only if all groups had a thorough knowledge of the problems to be met. Boat officers, in addition to learning the intricate codes set up for recognition and communication, became versed in the objectives of the troops they would carry in to the beaches. Troop officers, in the same way, studied the problems and methods of naval landing operations and fire support.

The actual rehearsal progressed smoothly. A delay in the lowering of landing craft from the transports caused Admiral Hill a few extra moments of pacing, but otherwise he had few criticisms. Troops clambered down nets and into the waiting landing boats. The first wave hit the beach, followed by the second and the third. Mock objectives were taken, and the island was rapidly secured. Enemy resistance, of course, was missing. Though it would be an unpredictable factor on D-day, the hours of planning and practice would cut later risk to a minimum.

We approached the island of Tarawa at midnight on November 19. The transports slid noiselessly through the calm, black water. Ship's company and troops crowded the weather decks, each man straining to see through the pitch-black darkness. Inside there were no lights except for dim red battle lamps marking the passageways. Ahead we could hear the muffled thunder of big guns. Faint streaks of light marked the flight of tracer shells. Star shells occasionally blossomed like Fourth of July sparklers, hung in the sky for a few moments, and then snapped out. It was like watching a faraway movie screen; the scene was wholly unreal and yet personal.

The transport area was several thousand yards from the shore. By the time we reached it, the ship was in a confusion of activity. Condition 1-A, the designation given to a ship's administration during loading and unloading operations, was set. Hatch covers were thrown off, booms were manned, and boats were lowered noisily to the water, where they chugged about the ship like baby ducklings. The public-address system blared forth all sorts of information. "Now MacAlister, seaman first class, lay up to number two hold on the double! . . . Now the boat crew of number fourteen boat, lay aft to debark five! . . . Will Lieutenant Jones please lay up to the troop commander's cabin!" There was a certain relief in activity. The tenseness of the approach gave way to the cheerfulness prevalent at the start of the trip.

The gunfire, once far away, was now close at hand. Battleships, cruisers, and destroyers lying-to beyond us lobbed their shells over our area. The whine of the five-inchers was occasionally interspersed with the chug-chug-whoosh of the big fellows.

All went according to schedule until about 0300. Then the Jap shore batteries opened up. Apparently their surface radar, if any existed, did not distinguish between fighting ships and auxiliaries. Three heavy shells landed off our port bow, a fourth passed between our stacks. Officers and men dived for cover. The narrow passageway entrances were jammed with men thinking of one thing, their own immediate safety.

Acting on orders, we rapidly retired from the transport area. Nerves remained jumpy. A three-inch shell lodged in one of our guns had to be fired. The sharp report came unexpectedly and the result was almost ludicrous. Men flattened themselves on the decks in layers up to three deep. One of the bosun's mates, Ed Buczek, jumped from the after hatch cover down through a two-foot escape hatch and into the laundry, a distance of at least fifteen feet. It was a shamefaced group that untangled itself.

Dawn finally broke over the scene. Pictures of the island, a low, coral-and-sand piece of wreckage, are now familiar to everyone. Once-stately palm trees now were grotesque and jagged stumps. The beach was pockmarked with shell holes. It seemed impossible that any life could still remain.

At 0630 we re-anchored in the debarkation area. By 0730 troops of the first wave were in the boats and heading shoreward in squadron formation.

"Tony," a low-flying naval observation plane, radioed steady reports of the progress. He described the slaughter of the men as they waded in from the reefs. From our ship we could see that our advance had been stopped in the central sector, and Tony told us why. "Tony calling . . . Tony calling . . . . Jap three-incher one hundred yards back of beach, sector two . . . the goddamn thing's killing our men . . . get on it . . . get on it!"

A few minutes later a destroyer slid in near the reef. There it lay, sending salvo after salvo into the area indicated by Tony. Tony again came back on the air. "Tony to DD . . . You did a damn good job!"

Whoever the pilot of Tony was, he had our respect. Again and again we saw him wheel around, dip down, and skim in barely one hundred feet above the ground. The air about him was alive with tracer bullets.

Our naval bombardment began again. This time the objectives were marked. After two hours of steady pounding, the Nip emplacements were sufficiently silenced to allow the effective landing of reinforcements.

Reports have told of the carnage of that landing and of the great losses to Marine personnel. But little has been said of the damage inflicted on the Navy-manned landing craft, tiny, slow-moving barges that clanked up onto the reefs to discharge the troops. Some managed to back down from the coral. Others, hung on the reefs, were blasted by machine-gun and mortar fire.

It took courage to man those boats. The troops were partially protected by the bulletproof ramp, but the boat officers and boat crews had to remain exposed in order to control the crafts. One coxswain returned to the ship and demanded to see the captain. "Captain," he reported, "my crew is scared . . . they're just kids. I'll have to have new men before I go out again." As his boat approached the reef, it had been caught in a steady stream of fire. His men, never exposed to gunfire before, dived for cover underneath the stern sheets. Singlehanded, the coxswain had maneuvered the boat into the beach, discharged his troops, and returned to the ship. The failure of his men might easily have lost the landing craft. Yet he excused them as being kids — and he himself was barely nineteen years old.

Before the landing Ensign Hugh Price, a Minneapolis boy, had admitted to many of us that he was worried. He had had no previous experience, and he was afraid that he might, as he expressed it, "turn chicken." It was with this feeling that he left the ship with the first wave. An hour later his boat pulled alongside the Doyen. Price was at the wheel. He shouted up to us, "It's the best damn fun I've ever had. Send me some chow. I'm heading back in."

The Doyen was fortunate. Though six of her boats were damaged, none of her men were lost. One youngster had the wheel shot from between his hands. He steered the boat by using the leverage provided by a Stillson wrench.

The day was not a pleasant one to remember. Within three hours of the initial landing attempt, boats were thumping alongside loaded with casualties. The booms were kept busy alternately discharging cargo and hoisting aboard the wounded.

Our beach party was sent ashore the morning of the second day. Lieutenant Commander Fabian, assistant to the executive officer, had gone ashore the day before to act as squadron beachmaster. He was to coordinate the supply lines to the beach and organize stowage and distribution of the items once they were landed.

Aboard ship Fabian was a quiet, unassuming sort of person, much more interested in the paper work of administration than in personal command. A returning Marine, however, described his work on the beach. "That guy Fabian is a madman. I saw him out on the pier, fussing like an old woman just because one boat was slow in unloading. There was enough lead flying around him to plate a battleship." Fabian was later awarded the Silver Star medal for conspicuous bravery under fire.

One member of the ship's beach party deserves special mention, though he received no official commendation and was almost court-martialed for desertion. Shipfitter Shain, finding the going not sufficiently exciting for his Irish temperament, loaded himself with grenades, shells, and a carbine, and joined a party of Marines. He neglected, however, to ask for permission. For three days he ate, slept, and fought with the front-line troops. When the most intense fighting was over, he was sent back to the ship. The officer under whom he had served sent with him a brief message addressed to the commanding officer. The message read, "Credit this man with three Japs killed." It was a good defense against any contemplated disciplinary action.

Tarawa is one of several islands in the Gilbert group. Though it was the most heavily fortified, the Japs had developed minor installations on some of the others. Late the second night an order was received for the Doyen to send in a group of scouts, Marines specially trained in reconnaissance work, to check the defenses of a small island about ten miles off our bow. The message specified that the scouts were to be landed by 2430, that the boats were to lie-to until 0430, and were then to carry the scouts back to the ship.

Owing to a delay in transmission, the order was not received until 0100. Ensigns Tom Hawk and Dan Minnich were chosen to command the group. Operating with four boats, Hawk and Minnich took their little division to within two thousand yards of the shore. Calculations were correct. They had approached silently and no counterfire had been experienced. Charts, checked by the muffled glow of flashlights, showed unobstructed water ahead. The boats pointed inland toward a small cove, with motors cut down to idling speed. In the meantime the scouts prepared to disembark. The small rubber boats were inflated, and the men smeared their faces with blacking. At that moment, the boats ran aground on a barely submerged, uncharted reef. The time was 0300. Tom managed to back his boat off the coral. For half an hour he attempted to find an opening into the cove, but it became evident that the cove could not be entered before high tide. The distance to the shore from the entrance of the cove was too great to be safely navigated by the rubber boats, and, since morning was approaching, the group returned to the ship.

Tom has since claimed that he owes his life to that reef. The following morning, Tony reported that four heavily armed Japanese barges were firing upon him from the cove.

Hawk and Minnich took the same group ashore on the third day. This time, however, the landing was made at a different point. The raiders split into two groups; one went down to the end of the v-shaped atoll, and the other hit at the halfway mark. Ashore, the Marines met with success. They secured several oil storage tanks intact and killed all the Japanese guards. The group was later commended by the commanding general of the Marine Corps.

For the Doyen the combat phase of the battle of Tarawa was over. Her shallow draft, however, singled her out as the only transport capable of safely entering the inner lagoon for the embarkation and treatment of casualties. Piloted by a bearded Englishman, a former resident of the Gilberts, she slid through the short stretch of water which seemed to us to be only inches deep. Each crisp command of the pilot was punctuated by the splat of chewing tobacco skillfully landed in a little tin cup that he carried with him.

For four days we lay at anchor, until almost four hundred wounded men had been taken aboard. The doctors, facing combat surgery for the first time, worked night and day. Operating rooms were improvised in both the upper and lower wardrooms. The decks and passageways were literally smeared with blood. Jim Oliver and Al Kelly handled the abdominal cases. Bob Watkins, former bone surgeon from San Francisco, took care of the fractures and amputations. The tireless corpsmen, helped by willing hands from the other divisions, did all that could be done for the men before and after treatment.

This was the part of the battle which brought home to us the ugly seriousness of war. Though the wounded men themselves could laugh about their recent experiences, it was difficult for any of us to appreciate the humor. One boy of eighteen, minus his right arm, told us how he had spent the previous night while he waited for the corpsmen to get to him. Laughing, he said, "I was lying in a foxhole and was getting thirsty as hell. Right outside, there was a dead Marine. I knew he wouldn't ever need his canteen. I started to crawl out after it, when zowie . . . some Jap sniper nicked my helmet. So I really fooled him. I lay down on my back, put my helmet on my foot, and every minute or so I stuck it up over the edge a few inches. I kept that bastard awake all night. It was sure fun while it lasted."

It was not a happy ship that finally sailed from Tarawa. Three hundred and eighty bunks were filled with wounded and crippled men. On the fantail were eight long canvas sacks, laid neatly side by side.

The eight dead Marines were buried at sea. The military service was brief and impressive.

It is difficult to describe the emotions we experienced. Youngsters, grown old, stood uncovered on the afterdeck. A steady rain splattered down upon us. In the stillness the soft voice of Chaplain Ingvoldstad was clearly heard:

"I am the Resurrection and the Life, saith the Lord: he that believeth in me, though he were dead, yet shall he live; and whosoever liveth and believeth in me, shall never die. . . .

"Unto Almighty God we commend the soul of our brother departed, and we commit his body to the deep; in sure and certain hope of the Resurrection unto eternal life, through our Lord Jesus Christ; at whose coming in glorious majesty to judge the world, the sea shall give up her dead; and the corruptible bodies of those who sleep in him shall be changed, and made like unto his glorious body; according to the mighty working whereby he is able to subdue all things unto himself."

A volley was fired, and the canvas-bound bodies slid gently into the sea.

The service itself was a form of action, a picture that moved steadily before us — the flag at half-mast, the prayer, the committal. But afterward, when we went one by one to our rooms, it was with a growing feeling of bitterness.

7. Pigeon Mates

"Hey, Major! Have you heard about the new shell the Navy has developed?" The speaker was our irrepressible Irishman, Timmins. As the Marine Corps major had no reply, Tim continued. "Well, after the Navy finishes shelling a place, they shoot over this special shell. When it explodes, it rams a staff into the ground and raises the American flag. The Marines don't have to go ashore at all!"

At the moment the Doyen was sitting eight miles off the islands of Roi and Namur in the Marshall Islands group. It was D-day plus two. So far, the job of taking the Marshalls seemed to be as easy as Timmins' yarn suggested. The high command, apparently learning a lesson from Tarawa, had subjected the islands to a week's steady bombardment. The first waves had met little resistance, and the project looked like a field day for our forces.

We had arrived at Kwajalein Atoll on D-day, January 31. We had come almost directly from the States, where after Tarawa all watches had had seventy-two-hour liberties in San Diego, and spirits were generally high. The crossing had been uneventful except for a few minor skirmishes between crew members and our passengers, the Fourth Marine Division, as yet untried in combat. All hands were treating the present engagement as a good-sized picnic.

Through field glasses we had been able to watch some of the action. On the first day underwater demolition teams, men especially trained in underwater swimming and blasting, had gone in to destroy reef barriers. One of the groups had swum clear in to a pier built by the Japanese. A small warehouse stood on the shore. The building was covered with large red crosses but it was obviously not being used for hospitalization. Charges were placed about the building, and the resulting explosion was the biggest we had ever seen, unbelievably big in relation to the size of the charges used. Though we were miles from the blast, the ship shuddered under the impact. Door curtains snapped; loose articles fell to the deck. Over on the beach flames and smoke spumed hundreds of feet upward. A huge white mushroom of smoke, as if blown by a giant, rose at least a mile into the air.

The explanation came by radio. Using the Red Cross insignia as camouflage, the Japs had stored torpedo warheads in the building.

On the third day our beach party was sent ashore. There was no difficulty in getting volunteers, for returning Marines had come aboard loaded down with Jap souvenirs. Every crew member was impatient for an opportunity to try his hand at collecting.

With the beach party ashore, it became necessary to send in food. Commander Schindler had managed to "borrow" a dozen five-gallon thermos jugs from the Army at Kiska. The jugs were filled with chile con carne, or with soup, or coffee. A number of men offered to take them over to the beach. Chief Commissary Steward Metras was insistent that he should be the man to go. Although the food was already prepared, he was certain that only he could properly supervise its transit. After some discussion, Metras, Parker, and Crawford loaded the rations into an LCVP, climbed in after them, and headed shoreward.

It was night before they returned. No explanation for the delay was offered, possibly because none existed. They probably felt that the day's vacation had been worth any subsequent punishment. Their boat looked like a backyard junk pile. Machine guns, swords, helmets, rifles, and shell casings littered the deck. Only its extreme size had prevented Crawford from bringing aboard the wing section of a Zero. Among the more interesting booty were Japanese army watches, poorly made affairs encased in locket-type mountings, and finely carved, silver-inlaid opium pipes.

Parker told me how they had found them. "We noticed that most of the Jap bodies had had their pockets cut away. If they were lying on their faces, their rear pants pockets were gone. If they were on their backs, their shirt pockets were gone. We thought for a while we weren't going to get anything. Then Crawford got a good idea. He took a stick and turned one of the bastards over. Sure enough, the Marines hadn't taken the time to do a complete job."

About the fifth day, the Doyen was ordered to take prisoners aboard. This was our first real contact with the enemy and most of us lined the rails as the boats approached.

In a way it was disappointing. The naked, bandy-legged soldiers looked more like boys than men. Most of them were Koreans, taken to Kwajalein Atoll to serve in labor battalions. At first, they showed fear and sullenness at being captured. Then, as they found they were not going to be hurt, many began to smile and jabber away at top speed. Our interpreter informed us that some of the men actually regarded us as liberators, and that, to a few of the better educated, San Diego and San Francisco represented a sort of Shangri-La.

The medical department and the master-at-arms took charge of them as they came aboard. First on the schedule came a thorough scrubbing. (The wounded, of course, were segregated for treatment.) A store-room, partitioned with metal fencing, was converted into a brig. All the able-bodied prisoners were herded into it. "Guards" were plentiful. Until the executive officer intervened, the prison space resembled a zoo on a public holiday. Our men crowded up to the entry to gape at the Japs, and the Japs, equally interested, stared back.

A near riot broke out toward morning. The guard reported that all had been orderly until 0300, when he had been startled by a muffled scream. Turning his battle lantern onto the prisoners, he had found them all huddled into one corner and very much awake. A hurried call brought more guards. They crashed into the cell, unpiled the prisoners, and down in the corner they discovered one of the Japs almost dead from strangulation.

After an interview with three of the inmates — the victim had refused to talk — the interpreter discovered that the injured man had been overseer of the labor battalion. A master sergeant in the Japanese army, he had always treated the Koreans as slaves. For his own protection, he was put in solitary confinement except during the working day, when he was allowed to swab down the large prison cell. Though the Koreans took evident delight in watching him perform such menial labor, the sergeant never gave any indication of annoyance. He went about his work stolidly, and with a thoroughness that was creditable.

Among the wounded prisoners were two members of the so-called Imperial Marines, the naval landing force. Though they were sworn to kill themselves rather than be captured, they had been so severely injured that suicide was impossible. The medical officers couldn't help admiring their courage. Doc Oliver pulled an inch-long fragment of shrapnel from the skull of one. It was deeply imbedded and the process must have been extremely painful, yet the man made no sign of discomfort. The other prisoner had a long open wound on his forearm. Tincture of iodine was poured into it. His only change in expression was an involuntary drawing in of breath.

The day after the prisoners were brought aboard, a photographer from a nationally known magazine arrived to photograph them. He skillfully lined up his pictures. In one of them, Pop Slattery, chief master at arms, was shown directing the Japs. The other shot was of the prison cell. When the pictures finally appeared in the magazine, the caption read: "Prisoners taken aboard Coast Guard manned ship at Marshalls." Coast Guard! And Pop with twenty-nine years in the Navy!

By February 9 the Marshalls were proclaimed secure. On that day we headed back for Pearl Harbor. The excitement wasn't quite over, however. The second day out a pigeon hovered over the signal bridge and then dropped exhausted onto the deck. Brusco, one of the signalmen, captured him for a pet. Upon close examination, he found a tube attached to the bird's leg. He excitedly called Bosun Trippler, and the two of them carried the bird to the intelligence officer. It was a Jap carrier pigeon. Where it was heading, or what was in the message, the officer would not divulge.

The fact of its capture was news. We had an Associated Press photographer aboard and his picture of Bosun Trippler holding the pigeon appeared in most of the nation's newspapers. The incident, however, was not properly appreciated by the principals involved. For weeks afterward they were known aboard the Doyen as Pigeon Mates Trippler and Brusco, the heroes of the Marshall Islands.

8. Time Out

With the completion of the Marshall Islands campaign came our first real taste of combat boredom, the kind of life that actually makes up the greater share of war. So far we had been kept continuously on the go, the week's layover in New Zealand having been our longest single stop. But on our return to the Hawaiian Islands we learned that we were scheduled to stay there for "an extended period," which, it turned out, was to be three and a half months.

The start of this period was marked by several changes in the officer personnel. Commander McClaughry had been made captain, and the post of executive officer was now filled by Lieutenant Commander Ralph Lane, formerly chief engineer. Warrant Officer Timmins had received a spot promotion to lieutenant junior grade and he took over Lane's job. Tall, scholarly "Big Joe" Donat, also a j.g., was appointed navigator. I was ordered to relieve Schindler as supply officer. These changes helped a little to lessen the monotony of the first weeks, at least for those of us who had new jobs to learn.

Then the days began to drag. They reminded me of the closing days of the year in grade school, those long, dull days that directly precede summer vacation. The ship was cleaned to a spit-and-polish perfection. But even so, it required only about two hours a day to keep it that way.

The first signs of the strain came suddenly. Late one afternoon a shore-patrol craft approached the ship. It bumped against the gangway landing and three crestfallen sailors were herded aboard. A chief master-at-arms followed them up the ladder to present the officer of the deck with a written complaint. I was serving as recorder at the time, and a copy was sent to me from the ship's office. From its rather muddled wording, it appeared that one of the sailors, placid, rotund Carpenter's Mate Clarence Schuette, had assaulted a young lady during the ferryboat run from the naval base to Ford Island. Schuette was called in to give his version.

The boys had been on the beach that afternoon consuming their full share of beer and sorghum liquor. By the time they reached the ferry, they were in exceedingly high spirits. Schuette, loaded down with packages, was the soberest of the group. In order to rest his bundles on the railing, he walked up to the forward end of the slow-moving boat and chose a spot right next to a group of Kanaka women. Ed Neal, one of the happy topers, saw a chance for a wonderful practical joke. Slipping behind the unsuspecting Schuette, he reached around him and gave one of the girls a tweak in her very vulnerable backside. The enraged girl swung swiftly around and slammed Schuette across the face with her well-filled handbag. He stumbled backward, tripped, and fell, showering the deck with his packages. A major riot was commencing when the shore patrol arrived and took over.

What should we do about it? Nothing. According to Courts and Boards, our legal Bible, there was no "intent" on Schuette's part, and we didn't care to search for any elsewhere.

Schuette's escapade was only the beginning. One of our storekeepers, Cliff Hanlin from Iowa, had just been rated a first class petty officer. As the competition had been tough, he was naturally proud of his accomplishment and lorded it a bit over his fellow workers. One morning he walked into the supply office to find a pennant, manufactured from the seat of a worn pair of dungarees, draped above his desk. On it was painted the insignia of a first class storekeeper with the caption: "Lest We Forget."

The Doyen, it soon appeared, had developed a lonely hearts' club. Our duties as officers included the boring task of censoring all mail. The average letter was spot read in order to detect security violations, but occasionally we would find one interesting enough to read fully. One morning's batch contained at least a hundred mimeographed questionnaires addressed to one hundred different girls. They contained such queries as these: Do you like to neck? If so, to what extent? And will you with me? What is your size? your height? your weight? your bust? your hips? It was too bad that we could never see the replies.

One of the colored stewards, also interested in romance, sent a more personal letter to a prospective acquaintance. The steward was a thin, stoop-shouldered, listless chap, black as ebony. But in his letter he described himself this way: "Ise tall and hansom, and Ise light tan."

Our first lieutenant, Stan Gay, was much interested in being promoted to the rank of lieutenant commander. He was a middle-aged man, a native of Virginia, and something of a character. So far in his Navy career he had always occupied billets that called for an officer above the rank of lieutenant. The fact that he had never been given that rank he chose to blame on the congressmen. "Larry, they're just a bunch of damn billy goats! There isn't a good one among 'em. For twenty years I've been voting the prohibition ticket, and they know it. It's all a conspiracy. Why, I remember old Senator McFar . . ."

So it went, day after day, at the dinner table. It was a natural setup for a good joke. With the help of elfish Ensign Norris, assistant communications officer, we typed up a fake ALNAV (the official communique of the Navy Department). It read that because of the surplus of high-ranking officers, promotions to the rank of lieutenant commander would be discontinued for the duration. In its place, a temporary rank of super lieutenant was being established. The collar insignia was to be a black oak leaf and the sleeve insignia two gold stripes separated by a narrow warrant officer's stripe. Advancements were to be via blanket promotion — two years' service as lieutenant was the minimum requirement.

Stan, of course, was one of the first to receive a copy of the ALNAV. It bothered him. Most of the officers at the dinner table were in on the hoax, and all joined in to give him a rough time. "Boy, Stanley, you're really due for that new promotion. But what'll we call you? Superman?"

Stan left the table without waiting for dessert. He went immediately to the executive officer. "Commander," he said, "they can't make me take that new rank, can they? I want the extra money, but I'll be damned if I'll be called Superman." Late that evening he was still stewing over it. "It's just a damn downright dirty conspiracy of those billygoats!" was his final conclusion. The odd part of the story is that rumors of the new rank spread throughout the entire Pacific fleet.

Constructive outlets for energy were, of course, encouraged. Chaplain Ingvoldstad had been replaced by energetic, bulldoggish Jesse Swinson. Chaplain Swinson had played professional baseball in his younger days — he was first baseman with the Boston Red Sox — and did his best to encourage athletics. Though the shipboard space was limited, he instituted a course in calisthenics and organized a boxing and wrestling team. He also started an intramural Softball tournament, pitting one division of the ship's personnel against another.

The Softball games stirred up a lot of interest, particularly when it was learned that there would be plenty of free beer. As the chaplain worded it in a ship's newspaper article, "There'll be a prize for the winner, and there'll be a prize for the loser ... in fact, there'll be the same prize for everybody." One game was described in the paper as follows: "The port and starboard ball clubs, their espirit-de-corp boundless from twelve cases of beer, slugged it out for five innings. Meanwhile, Fireman Houston lighted off. Cook Smitty, 'Flunky' Scroggins, and 'Teetotaller' Bedell peeled onions and fried hamburgers over the open camp fire. When the port watch complained of darkness at the end of the fifth inning, Umpire McDonald, who hadn't seen a pitch since Crawford's seven walks in the first of the third had driven him to drink, was glad to call the game. Result? Port — 9; Starboard — 8."

Two of the officers, Tom Hawk and Bob Watkins, former bone surgeon from California, developed their own brand of entertainment. The shallow reefs offered good shell hunting, and Bob and Tom went in for it on a large scale. They constructed diving helmets from gas masks and were able to work even the outlying reefs. They brought back giant clams, some of them three feet in diameter, spider shells, and all sorts of coral formations. Of all their booty, "cat's eyes" were the best. A certain variety of snail possesses a calcareous growth at the end of its "foot." When the animal withdraws into its shell, this stone-like disc acts as a door. Depending on the location and feeding habits of the snail, the discs vary in color from eyelike mixtures of brown and white to combinations of deep green, brown, and white. Tom, in particular, did a thriving trade in them. A born merchant, he placed them on sale at sixty-five cents apiece.

Though shell collecting may have been popular with the hunters, it was not with the rest of us. Most of the animals were alive when they were brought aboard, and the process of cleaning them was a smelly one. Tom was my roommate, and for weeks our room stank like a bone fertilizer plant. One night a half dozen of Tom's shells disappeared. The thief, apparently wanting a few souvenirs for himself, hid them behind a ventilator intake. The result was more than he had anticipated: The commanding officer ordered a search of the ship — to make certain that there were no dead stowaways in any of the holds.

Toward the close of the three-month waiting period, I received my own initiation in shipboard humor. We had gone on a trial run and had anchored in a port in one of the larger Hawaiian Islands. Four of us went ashore for a sightseeing trip. Since we had leave papers, we were able to rent a U-Drive-It car from an automobile agency. It was registered in my name. That evening we stopped off at an officers' club at one of the near-by base hospitals. The liquor and the company were good, and the time passed rapidly. When the club closed, we discovered that it was 2215 — a quarter of an hour after the curfew on the island. The Army officers told us, however, that we would be able to drive back to the ship provided we kept our lights out. "As you leave the gate," they added, "the sentry will ask your names. Give 'em bogus ones. They'll never check up, and then you can be sure of not getting into any trouble."

Had we been cold sober, we would probably have questioned that advice, but at the time it sounded good. Sure enough, we were stopped as we left the grounds. I gave my name as: "Cedric B. Oswold . . . B as in bastard"; Long John Barber, "Hubert B. Carver ... B as in bastard"; Bob Royston, "Henry B. Huxley ... B as in bastard"; and Tex Wolford, "J. B. Brewster ... B as in bastard."

In spite of the unusual similarity in our middle initials, the sentry gave no sign of suspicion. The muffled laughs from the front and back seats didn't seem to bother him; he merely recorded the names given, but he also marked down the license number of the car. We rolled slowly toward the dock. The cool night air gradually began to have effect, and by the time we reached the entrance, we were beginning to regret our action.

Long John growled out the joint opinion. "Damn! We shouldn't have done it. What do you say we drive back to the hospital and square things away?" But Bob pointed out that maybe the Army officers had given us correct advice — maybe the names wouldn't be checked. It was now almost midnight, and if we did go back, we would probably be picked up by the military police for being on the road at that hour. We left the car at the dock, to be called for by an attendant from the agency, and went aboard ship.

The next morning we sailed for Pearl Harbor. We had barely docked when the guard mail was brought aboard. A few minutes later a messenger brought an envelope to my office, and in it was a copy of the following letter:

P22/A-8/204 May 21, 1944
Ser. 109
From: Commanding Officer,
U.S. Army 120th Station Hospital
APO, San Francisco, California
To: Commanding Officer, U.S.S. Doyen
Subject: Misconduct of Officer Personnel.

1. There has come to the attention of this command a matter of disciplinary importance which, because it apparently involves the question of moral turpitude, must necessarily be referred to you for action.

2. A sentry on duty at the gate of this base has reported that on the night of May 20th, 1944, at approximately 2215, a tan-colored Chevrolet five passenger sedan attempted to pass out of the gate. Acting in the line of duty, the sentry halted the vehicle, noting that its presence at that hour was in violation not only of this command's local regulations regarding curfew, but also in violation of the General Order promulgated some time ago for the entire Hawaiian area by General Richardson. The automobile bore a registration marker "K3455" and was at that time operated by a Naval officer who gave his name as "Cedric B. Oswold." The names of the other occupants of the vehicle were also noted by the sentry.

3. Further investigation at the automobile agency, however, revealed that that particular machine had been rented to a Lieut. Lawrence A. Marsden, attached to your command, and not to any "Cedric B. Oswold." Our records fail to reveal any Lieut. Marsden in the party involved. Hence, it appears reasonable to assume that the names given by the other occupants were also spurious.

4. Inasmuch as this, in the eyes of this command, is a serious offense, not only from the standpoint of curfew violation, but also from the angle of willfully and deliberately evading proper reply to challenge by an authorized sentry, this office passes this matter on for whatever action may be deemed appropriate.

Col. T. F. Gallagher, U.S.A. (Ret).

Copy to:

Lieut. Marsden

Bureau of Naval Personnel

I immediately called Long John and handed him the letter. The look on his face was one of surprise and disbelief. "It's a fake, Larry. It's a fake. That was the 179th hospital. That is ... I believe it was." By this time his hands were shaking so badly that the letter slipped to the deck. "My God," he continued, "if that letter's the straight dope, we'll get a general court-martial."

"What do you mean we!" I interjected. "My name is the only one they have."

"If you get stung, we'll stick by you. They'll have to try us all!" John thought for a moment; all the color had drained from his face. "Who signed that letter?" he asked. We looked. "T. F. Gallagher . . . why I'll bet that's old Teddy Gallagher, a friend of my father when he was in the Army medical service. Dad used to say he was the toughest man on discipline he ever met. Larry, we've got to do something about this right away!"

That evening four anxious men went to the executive officer's room. Commander Lane, a bull-like, powerful man, with one of the keenest intellects of any officer I have known, gave us little consolation. "Giving wrong names to a sentry is pretty serious. I ran into a little trouble myself on the same grounds . . . but that was years ago in San Diego. Maybe I can do something for you. The district disciplinary officer is a good friend of mine and I imagine that all letters of this type go through him before copies are forwarded to the Bureau of Naval Personnel. I'll try to see him tomorrow. Maybe he can help."

Though the next day was a busy one, the hours dragged by. Commander Lane returned aboard to inform us that his friend was away. We were a worried group. Long John was even contemplating suicide rather than face dishonor. (He later received the Bronze Star for heroism under fire at the landing at Makin Island.)

The executive officer finally contacted his friend by telephone. On the afternoon of the twenty-fourth he called us up to his cabin and informed us that the entire matter was squelched. Gratefully we filed into the upper wardroom. John broke the silence. "I think we all ought to chip in five dollars apiece and buy the commander a present." I agreed. Bob, however, objected.

"Fellows," he argued, "that's against Navy Regs . . . and besides, he didn't do anything for me ... I would never have admitted being in that car. The only guy that benefited was Larry." John and I were speechless. Tex then added his opinion.

"I suggest we show our appreciation in a different way. Let's do what he wants when he wants it done . . . let's really show him we're 100 per cent behind him." This suggestion was acceptable to all.

The next forenoon Mr. Lane walked into the wardroom and casually suggested that the life rafts be inspected. Long John jumped to his feet. "Yes sir, Commander. Right away, sir!" He was gone in two strides of his long legs.

Two weeks later Tex and Bob came to my cabin. "Larry," Tex began, "do you have a good sense of humor?"

"I guess so," I replied.

"Well," continued Tex, "that letter from Colonel Gallagher . . . Bob and I made it up . . . and Mr. Lane helped!"

If a man doesn't have a good sense of humor when he comes aboard ship, he'll develop one — he'll have to.

9. Saipan

He waddled drunkenly across the deck. Though he reeked of the beer he had been drinking, no one seemed to mind. Even Captain McClaughry laughed as he watched him. The toper was Siwash, the drunken duck, mascot of the Second Marines.

It was June 5, 1944, and the Doyen was again plowing westward on a pay run. Where we were heading had not yet been revealed. It was believed, of course, that the ultimate goal of the high command was China. But whether we would reach it via the Marianas, Truk, or the Philippines was still a question. The Pacific was anybody's ocean. Though we had established bases in the Marshalls and the Gilberts, four thousand miles of ocean remained to be neutralized — four thousand miles of water pockmarked by Japanese strongholds.

I doubt that anyone was optimistic. Allied reconnaissance had clearly shown the defensive and offensive strength of Truk. It was known that the Marianas had been heavily fortified. Since it was hardly conceivable that we should attempt to by-pass both these places, we were certain that one of them was to be our objective.

Some of the men took advantage of this uncertainty, at the expense of one of the masters-at-arms.

At the time the Doyen went into commission, many of her crew had been temporarily quartered at the naval operating base at Terminal Island. Some of them, like Ace Parker, Crawford, Hayes, and Haug, were already veterans of Guadalcanal. Nonetheless, they were all subject to the strict disciplinary rules of the shore base. On one occasion Parker, Crawford, and Hayes, all petty officers, were standing near one of the buildings. Around the corner whipped a seaman first class, wearing the badge of a master-at-arms. "Attention, you men!" the youngster shouted. "Square those shoulders . . . pull in those guts . . . throw those cigarettes away!" Like small-town dignitaries being bawled out by city police, the surprised P.O.'s did as they were told. But they didn't like it. Afterwards they asked the name of their assailant, who was well known on the base for this sort of thing. Just before we left Pearl Harbor a draft of men was ordered aboard.

And in that draft was the former master-at-arms, Seaman First Class Figueroa.

Figueroa received a thorough initiation. From the moment he crossed the gangplank, he received the full attention of Parker, Crawford, and Hayes. These three, now chief petty officers, knew that he had never been in battle before and they proceeded to prepare him for the worst. By the third day out the poor fellow was eating, working, and sleeping in his life-jacket and helmet.

At 1000 on the morning of the fourth day we were called to quarters. It was unexpected, and as we walked back toward the main deck aft we wondered why. Just before we had sailed from Pearl Harbor, Commander Lane had been replaced by a fiery, young newcomer, 27-year-old Lieutenant Commander Daniel Hogan. Commander Hogan called us to attention, and, as we assembled in a u-shaped formation, he read off the following names: "Lieutenant Commander James B. Oliver, Lieutenant Albert C. Kelly, Lieutenant Robert P. Watkins, and Lieutenant John R. Barber. Will you please step forward." The four men formed a line facing the commander, and an orderly was then sent for Captain McClaughry. When the captain arrived, it was obvious that he was pleased. Addressing us, he announced, "It is my privilege to award the following medals: To Doctor Oliver, the Legion of Merit for the exemplary performance of his duties at Tarawa; to Doctor Kelly and to Doctor Watkins, the Bronze Star for their services at Tarawa; and to John Barber, the Bronze Star for heroism at the landing on Makin Island." We were all as proud as the actual recipients. It meant that the Doyen, too, had done a good job.

Two weeks of steady sailing brought us to the Marshalls. There, in a well-protected lagoon, the Navy had established an extensive supply depot. While the ship fueled and provisioned, operational plans were at last broken out.

We found that we were attached to Task Force 51; that we were scheduled to hit Saipan in the Marianas; that four days after our initial assault a southern group would attack Guam. It seemed to us a formidable schedule. We thought of the Jap fleet stationed at Truk; of the enemy airfields scattered throughout that area; of the land-based planes from the Marianas, the Volcanos, the Ryukyus, and the Bonins.

Under way again. If we were nervous, our passengers were not. Marine Private Earl Hall, ex-burlesque comedian from the East Coast, whipped up a lusty show. Assisted by Nat Berman, a former Walt Disney cartoonist, the boys worked up a song-and-dance recital complete with grass skirts and makeshift brassieres. Skits were numerous. Though the program would never have passed the Hays office, it did serve the purpose of getting laughs. Hall and Berman kept up the good work night after night until Berman came down with a severe case of mumps. He told everyone, confidentially, that he had carried the germs with him for months. He had just waited until the right time to use them.

Since the days of "Torpedo Junction," Japanese submarines had rarely been heard from. Though intelligence reports showed a great many contacts throughout the Pacific, we had read of no attacks. Then one night my roommate, Keith Petty, awakened me. "Larry . . . listen!" His tone was so intense that I half thought the ship had been hit. At first I could hear nothing. Then a thudding became audible. The sound, something like a muffled kettledrum, was regular in its cadence. "Depth charges," Keith whispered, "like we heard at Kiska." Movements in the passageway indicated that others had noticed the noise. We dressed quickly and hurried into the upper wardroom, where the other officers had already gathered. Swaddled in our kapok jackets, we sat around for forty-five minutes until word was received from the signal bridge that all was clear. The next morning a full report was given. Three subs had attempted to ambush our convoy, but the quick action of the destroyers and destroyer escorts had frightened them away. Only two "fish" had been released, and they had been poorly aimed.

Tokyo Rose did her best to worry us. As we finally approached the Marianas, she announced in a theatrical voice, "You men of the United States are now crossing over some of the deepest water in the Pacific. Think for a moment. Directly below you, the waters drop for seven miles . . . down . . . down . . . down where all is inky blackness . . . where ships and bones remain suspended in the black depths. Do you want that place of horror to be your grave? Turn back now, for if you don't, it will be too late."

Rose had one avid listener. He was Lil Edmonson, an eighteen-year-old colored steward. His eyes fairly bugged as he listened to the words pour out of the wardroom loudspeaker. Ten minutes later I overheard him giving the text of the message to one of his friends. The two of them were standing on the starboard weather deck, staring with awe at the placid ocean. "Jus' think, Hosie," Edmonson began, "this here water is seben mile deep . . . seben mile . . . straight down." Then with great conviction he exclaimed, "An' this here's only the top!"

D-day at Saipan was June 15, 1944. A reporter for the National Geographic once wrote that Saipan and Tinian were the two most beautiful islands in the world. As we watched the land grow steadily larger, we could understand why he thought so. Although mountainous, much of the island was under cultivation. From the small town of Garapan, we could see a broad, paved road winding back into the hills. The terrific naval bombardment then going on had leveled most of the shoreline trees. Garapan was reduced to piles of adobe and stone. To the far right, like a grotesque Picasso symbol, stood the smokestack of a sugar refinery. It seemed incongruous that a war should be taking place on this land meant only for beauty.

At approximately 0930 the first wave went in. Though opposition was met — mortar fire directed at the landing craft and at the shore — the first contingent of Marines secured their beachhead with relatively small losses. The regular radio reports indicated that the bulk of the Jap defenders had moved inland up into the hills.

We watched the planes attempt to blast out a pocket of resistance. One by one they swooped down almost to treetop level before dropping their bombs. Antiaircraft fire was strong. The pilot of a Hellcat located a mortar emplacement. Twice he dove at it, and both times he was driven away by counterfire. The third time he took his plane up to about three thousand feet. Falling into a slow, shallow dive, he pointed directly at his target. We could see him getting nearer and nearer. He dropped his bombs from less than one hundred feet. When the smoke of the explosion cleared away, both gun emplacement and plane had been destroyed.

The day passed uneventfully. Reconnaissance group number one, composed of the same personnel we had carried as Marine raiders at Tarawa, was taken ashore, and we were left with little to do except observe. Reports continued to be favorable; there was no evidence of enemy aircraft.

At midnight general quarters was sounded. Sleepy men piled onto the decks. The passageways sounded with the excited trampling of feet. Each of us wondered what had caused the alert. Up in the communications office we were able to hear the reports as they came in. "Bogies seventeen miles heading north by east." How many they were or what they were we did not know. The com shack was small and hot; it was difficult to think sensibly.

I wanted suddenly to be outside; the room felt like a trap. It was easy to visualize planes overhead, and the long downward sweep of their bombs. Seventeen miles. That meant less than ten minutes to wait.

Keith Petty and I slid open the door and climbed the ladder to the superstructure deck. Overhead the sky stretched quietly away. Though the moon had not risen, the light from the stars silhouetted the hundreds of ships around us. The usual thoughts flashed through my mind. "Wonder how much of a target we make from above . . . there's a lot of ships here . . . our odds of getting hit should be pretty slim. Can't hear any planes . . . maybe the radar isn't working right . . . maybe they've turned back . . . the sky's too peaceful . . ."

Ssssssshhhhwooosh. Ssssssshhhhwoooosh. Ssssssshhhhwoooosh. Three bombs landed in the water about 150 yards off our port side. It was a moment before we realized what had happened. Then we hit the deck! Tom Hawk, coming forward from the fantail when the explosions came, dived for a gun tub, only to find the deck already piled with men. Over the loud speaker came the excited voice of the executive officer, "All hands prepare for bombing attack! All hands take cover!" Psychologically, this was an unfortunate announcement. We were just plain scared. The gun crews could see nothing in the blackness. The passageways were jammed with excited men. A fourth bomb landed on the beach. Then the planes, high-altitude bombers, had passed over.

The next morning we saw part of the reason for the midnight attack. Four Japanese coastal vessels had attempted to land reinforcements, but all four had run head-on into two destroyers, one of them the U.S.S. Shaw. The Shaw, which had been in dry dock in Pearl Harbor the morning of December 7, 1941, had evened the score. The Jap ships lay partially submerged near the shore.

It was interesting to hear the Nipponese version of what was taking place. Perhaps it was a stratagem of the Japanese island commander at Saipan, perhaps the usual propaganda attempt at bolstering homefront morale. Whatever the reason, Radio Tokyo babbled steadily away. Three days before the initial landing, it was reported that the "defenders of Saipan had repulsed the American raiders with great losses to the enemy." On D-day Tokyo Rose admitted we had landed, but added that we would be "thrown from the beaches by sundown." Still optimistic on D-day plus two, she stated that "the Americans had advanced somewhat, but were paying a tremendous price." Most impressive was her list of our ships, from battlewagons and carriers down to small landing craft, that had been sunk by Jap coastal artillerymen and aviators. To this list was added the American fleet units destroyed by the "far-ranging" flyers from the Volcanos, Bonins, and Ryukyus. It was obvious that only remnants of Task Force 51 remained.

The strange thing about all this was that the commander of the Jap fleet units, making a sortie from behind the Philippines, believed these reports, and laid his plans accordingly. He arrived at what could have been an excellent plan. Confident that the American battle units had been destroyed, he chose as his objective the destruction of the supposedly helpless fleet of transports. He launched his carrier-based aircraft from their maximum range of six hundred to seven hundred miles. The plan was for the planes to pull another Pearl Harbor, land on the fields of Guam and Saipan for refueling, and return to their carriers in plenty of time to guard against any attacks the "remnants" of our fleet might attempt.

The Saipan commander, however, failed to notify the homefront, or anyone else, that the Saipan airfields were then in our hands, that the fields at Guam were completely unserviceable, or that hundreds of American carrier planes were circling the islands.

It is easy to imagine the shock the Jap fleet commander must have had when his planes failed to return. Apparently he guessed what had happened, for he wheeled his task group around and headed for safer waters. All the time, our patrol planes and subs were tailing his fleet, and Halsey and his "dirty tricks" gang were steaming at maximum speed to catch it. Halsey succeeded in inflicting serious blows on the partially defenseless Japs, but he was unable to deliver a really crushing attack. The wind was from the east, and in order to launch or recover planes, the entire disposition had to be turned from the westward chase into the wind, thus losing precious hours. The Japs build fast ships, and the margin gained by this delay was sufficient to allow them to escape.

By noon of the second day the Nips commenced a strong counterattack on Saipan. Using their tank-supported infantry, they succeeded in recapturing a plain just above Garapan. Loss of life was heavy. Our beach party, under the command of Lieutenant John Keogh, was sent ashore to help organize supply and aid in the evacuation of the wounded.

About 1500 one of the gun lookouts reported a body off the stern. We could see it floating, barely awash. Spread-eagled head down on the water, it bobbled slowly up and down. A boat was dispatched to bring it in.

Through the glasses, we watched the men as they attempted to grapple it with boat hooks. Perhaps all of us were morbidly curious, for when the body was at last recovered and lifted over the side, the decks were packed with onlookers. It was unrecognizable, except for the Marine uniform. The water had softened the skin tissue; the natural pigment was gone, and the color remaining was curd-white with an occasional splotch of brown. Identification was impossible. The hands were too deteriorated for finger-printing. Though the dentist recorded the teeth formation, the type of filling was not sufficiently unusual to be of much help. It was difficult to regard this bloated piece of meat as a man. The captain sent for the sailmaker.

Casualties began to come aboard, and with them, stories of the fighting on the beach. We heard one story of a tank gunner whose machine had stalled on the crest of a rise overlooking the Jap front line: how the Japs set up gun after gun to blast the tank, how the gunner waited until the emplacement had been completed before he opened fire, and how the gunner muttered just before he pulled the trigger, "You believe you is . . . you ain't!"

On the fourth day a Chamorro mother and her baby boy were brought aboard. Both had been wounded. The woman's arm was badly shattered, and the boy had been hit in the stomach. She had undoubtedly been told of the savagery of the Americans, for as we hoisted her aboard, she clung fiercely to her child, almost defying us to touch either of them. Within fifteen minutes, though, she learned that she was among friends. One of the officers gave up his room, the mother was quickly tucked in bed, and the baby was bathed and bandaged. Chief Commissary Steward Metras took over at that point. Father of three children, he was adept at nursing. First he ladled out a bowl of soup. The mother appeared to enjoy it. Next came chocolate milk, and judging from the pleased expression on her face, it was the finest drink she had ever tasted. The ice cream, however, finally clinched the friendship!

For two days the mother and her child remained with us. In that time they grew used to the friendly onlookers who crowded their doorway at all hours of the day. We wondered what the war had meant to her. It was probable that her husband had been killed. If she had lived in the city, her home was gone. True, she was part of the enemy, yet we knew that she had taken no part in provoking this trouble. We were all sorry when word was received that the base hospital facilities were ready to accept civilians.

It was on the sixth day that one of the decisive shore battles was fought. Early in the morning the Japs sent a group of thirty tanks to retake a Yank-held plateau. It was a typical Banzai raid. The enemy, making no attempt at silence or surprise, aimed a power attack toward our lines. The tactic was poor, for the oncoming machines loomed as good targets for our antitank gunners. In three hours twenty-eight of the tanks had been knocked out.

A captain, returned as a casualty, told us an unusual part of the story. He was in command of the defenders. As the Japs approached, he passed the word for the gunners to fire, and, acting on his own orders, he fixed an antitank grenade to his rifle, lifted it out of the foxhole, and aimed it at an approaching tank. But before he could fire, a stray bullet detonated the charge. There was an explosion, strong enough to dismember a steel machine, barely two feet in front of him.

Hours later he regained consciousness. He was totally deaf but could communicate by pad and pencil. His men told him what had happened. Assuming that he was dead, they had phoned back for a replacement. Another captain was sent forward but was killed enroute. In the meantime the Jap advance had swept through the sector, and it took forty-five minutes of bitter counterattack to drive them back.

Equally strange was the penciled story of another officer. Walking along with his unit, he suddenly felt as if someone had hit him on the neck with a rock. He put his hands up to feel, and brought them away covered with blood. He had been shot through the neck with a small caliber bullet. An eighth of an inch either way and he would have been killed. As it was, all he suffered was an enforced period of silence.

By the eighteenth the job was over for most of the transports. The heavy casualties had caused a delay in the Guam invasion, so there were more than enough ships left to act as hospitals.

We were glad to head homeward, for the word was rapidly going around that we were scheduled for an immediate overhaul in the States.

10. Akimoto and Shiba

We were met at the dock in Pearl Harbor by a Marine band and three representatives of the Amphibious Command. Within two hours the entire personnel knew that our overhaul had been postponed — until after the next operation, Captain McClaughry assured us — and that we were to reload immediately for the assault on Guam. We felt like a badly mauled prizefighter when he hears the gong of a new round.

Four days later, on July 8, we headed west. Retracing the route we had followed to Saipan, we arrived at Guam on the twenty-second, D-day plus one.

The amphibious assault on Guam was easy compared with the action at Saipan. Although the troops met increased resistance as they drove inland, the fleet units were seldom called even to general quarters. Casualties were light and only a few of the transports were needed for hospital ships. Six days later, when our unit retired, the Doyen was ordered to carry prisoners of war.

Our prisoners consisted of two bewildered Jap infantrymen. One was a Jap regular, an infantry warrant officer with eleven years of service in China and Manchuria. He was short, about five-feet-four, but well-proportioned and beautifully muscled. He had worked his way up through the ranks, had been wounded and decorated with the Order of the Single Ray of the Rising Sun. He was precise, intelligent, and a model of discipline.

While he was being brought aboard, via our casualty block and tackle rig, he looked up at the five hundred men lined along the rail, all eagerly trying to get a glimpse of a real, live Jap.

You can't really hate people, I suppose, until you have had more intimate contact with them than we in the Navy had with the enemy. Ship against ship or plane against ship has a tinge of unreality about it that in no way resembles the intimacy of the man-to-man and hand-to-hand situations arising with the ground forces. So I don't believe this Jap was looking up into a sea of obviously or viciously hostile faces, but we could plainly see that he expected the worst. Every muscle and vein stood out on his body.

Inside him there must have been extreme fear and apprehension, yet he never winced.

He got off the stretcher, looked around, and saw Commander Hogan coming toward him. He snapped to attention and bowed stiffly from the waist, not so much in a gesture of humiliation or obeisance as in plain acknowledgment that he had been vanquished and was at our disposal. He was neither humble nor insolent; in fact, his manner was distinguished by a complete lack of any discernible emotion. All connection with the past had been completely blanked off and the future was a wholly unknown quantity. As he gradually realized that he would not be keelhauled on the spot, he appeared to relax a bit.

In the meantime, the second prisoner came aboard. He was as different from the warrant officer as a new recruit is from a Prussian general. This one was a buck private named Shiba, who had been in the army a little over a year. Obviously the last scraping from the Jap manpower barrel, he was a bare five feet tall and couldn't have weighed more than one hundred pounds soaking wet. The moment he hit the deck, he wasted no time looking for any such thing as a senior officer. He started bowing to everyone and anyone as fast as his torso could get parallel to the deck and back up again.

He was such an odd-looking fellow, more like a little monkey than anything as personal as a human being, that in the eyes of everyone aboard ship the connection he had with the Jap army immediately disappeared. All we could see was this queer little man vigorously bowing to one and all. The whole crew began laughing, and Shiba instinctively knew that people who could be laughing had, at least momentarily, forgotten any such designs as cutting out his heart. Having hit upon the key to that laughter, he renewed his bowing with even more vigor. His broad grin revealed a series of gold teeth in the best cartoonist version of the little Nipponese.

Shiba and Akimoto were then led to the sick bay for examination and a bath. Akimoto, the trained soldier, was put under a shower and automatically took his bath in the manner of a man who has been taught the value of water in warfare. He stood squarely under the shower head, gave the faucet a quick turn, received a shot of water and then promptly turned it off. Shiba, when he was led under it, turned on the water and would have stayed there all day had it not been turned off for him.

There was little to do on our return trip, so we had plenty of time for interrogating our prisoners. It offered the opportunity for an insight into the

Jap soldier's mind that is rarely presented. We had several excellent Japanese-English dictionaries on board, and one in particular, a glossary of military terms and expressions, proved invaluable. After four or five days, with the aid of gestures, line drawings, and word-pointing, an intelligent, if belabored, exchange of ideas was possible.

Shiba turned out to be thoroughly happy-go-lucky. He had no interest in being a soldier, was unmarried, and was convinced that Japan had lost the war. He had started out for Saipan three different times and each time had been sunk by one of our subs. He told us that in Japan they were saying you could walk from Singapore to Nagasaki on the hulls of American submarines.

In about three days Shiba started asking questions about San Francisco and what the prospects there would be after the war. When asked if he wanted to return to Japan, he broke out in a hearty guffaw which plainly said, "Do you think I'm crazy?" He was about thirty-one years old, though he looked nearer twenty-one. A draftsman by profession, he was quite apt at drawing. We kept him supplied with pencil and paper, and he drew all day long, copying from magazines or drawing his impressions of anything in which his captors indicated any interest.

He was given a dictionary and was soon writing our alphabet and copying and learning the meanings of many simple words. The guards, for something to do, began giving him lessons in English, which he absorbed with amazing rapidity. His former life seemed completely forgotten, and he was only interested in preparing himself for the new world to come. He had no idea what its shape would be or just where he would fit in, but he did realize that it wouldn't hurt him to know English.

Akimoto, on the other hand, was inclined to be morose and listless. He had been in the army too long and had been too intimately connected with Japan's expansion — he had joined the army in 1933 — to cast off his nationalism in a few days. He was a real soldier and exemplified all that was best, from a military view, in a Japanese fighting man. He certainly would have committed hara-kiri had he not been knocked unconscious. He told us that under the Japanese military code, failure to commit suicide to avoid capture is pardonable only if the soldier is unconscious, and even then quite a stigma is attached to it. After the war, when he went back to Japan, he would have to go before a military tribunal and explain all the circumstances surrounding his capture. If the tribunal did not believe his story or if they decided he had been negligent, he would be ordered to commit hara-kiri.

One of the Japanese words we learned was the word for foolish or absurd; it was, spelled phonetically, bakarashi. When Akimoto told us of the rules surrounding hara-kiri, we exclaimed this word with appropriate gestures. He agreed, but indicated that he had little to say in the matter. We explained that there would be a new set of military customs in Japan after the war, and that they certainly would not include anything so silly as suicide. He was greatly relieved and from then on seemed to take a new interest in life. Akimoto had a wife and two small children in Japan, and indicated that he wanted to return to them after the war.

Never having been taught how to act when captured, inasmuch as the Nipponese high command never discussed the possibility of a good soldier's being taken alive, he willingly answered any questions without the slightest attempt at deception. His answers may have been colored by Japanese propaganda, but he gave us the best information he knew. As a captured soldier, he automatically regarded himself as completely at our disposal.

Akimoto told us, for instance, that there were twenty-five thousand naval landing force troops at Truk, and that they were fairly well supplied by submarines, a fact which helped to account for the seeming inactivity of the Jap submarine fleet. He gave his estimate of the size of the garrisons at Saipan, Guam, Tinian, Rota, Pagan, the Philippines, and so on. Events proved his figures to have been correct within 10 per cent in almost every case.

We asked him how many aircraft carriers were left, and he replied that he did not know. When we asked him to estimate, he began laborious mental calculations accompanied by expressive facial contortions. We could almost see him reaching back in his memory to recall newspaper or other accounts of launchings, stories he had heard, and carriers he himself had seen. He very carefully added all these, and announced a figure that differed by only two from the figures listed by our Naval Intelligence.

How the prisoners could eat! Instructions are to treat them as decently as is compatible with operational conditions. Such handling makes the real job of interrogation much easier for Naval Intelligence interpreters. At any rate, these two ate as if they had never seen so much food before and thought it unlikely that they would ever see so much again. Everyone wanted to feed them ice cream just to watch their reactions. They were given enough to swim in.

They were taken out on deck for an hour in the morning and an hour in the afternoon to stretch their legs and exercise if they chose to. Akimoto, the muscle man, went through his own routine of body-building exercises each period. They were not unlike those used at our training camps. In addition, he had some neck-bending and stretching drills that accounted for his size nineteen neck. In fact, his head almost merged into his shoulders.

Little Shiba attempted to imitate Akimoto 's exercises, but he could never put his heart or his mind into it. An arm would go out very haphazardly, or he'd do half a leg squat, and then laugh sheepishly. The Japanese-English dictionary listed the various orders for the Jap manual of arms and parade ground drills. Commander Hogan ran them through it every day or so. Shiba enjoyed doing it because he knew we all got a kick out of watching him; Akimoto enjoyed it because he was a soldier through and through and liked anything connected with his former life. He was proud of his own perfection of execution.

We finally arrived at Pearl Harbor, where interpreters met the ship. Both the prisoners enjoyed the opportunity of conversing in their native tongue, and you could hardly stop them once they began. Akimoto was quite a prize. As an army man of long standing and a veteran of the Chinese theater, he was able to give information on the deployment of various army units in China and Manchuria. Having been well treated and anxious to do anything that might continue such treatment, he talked and talked.

Shortly before the prisoners left the ship, Akimoto formally expressed his thanks to the captain and to the chief master-at-arms, who had been in direct charge of him. He said he was sorry for having caused us any trouble. Shiba, the little monkey-faced private, was obviously sorry to go. As he walked across the deck, escorted by a Marine guard, he bowed to everyone he saw, saying over and over again, "Saaank Oooo . . . Saaank Oooo."

11. Change of Plans

"Hey, Lefty, what's the latest dope?" Lanky Beachmaster Keogh looked up from his chair at the speaker. "I don't know, Stan, what is it?"

"Well, I just heard over on the beach that the Doyen was ..."

And so it went. In the C.P.O. quarters, the crew's living compartments, and the wardroom, stories were flying thick and fast about the next operation. It was September 2, and we had just finished loading elements of the 96th Army Division, a group fresh from the States. Anyone's speculation was good as to where we were taking them.

It wasn't until the fifteenth that we finally got under way. All of us knew by that time that this next push was to be a big one; never before had we seen so many transports assembled. On the first day out from Pearl Harbor the word was passed over the loudspeaker. "The Doyen is to take part in the assault on the island of Yap in the Pelew group."

Charts were broken out, and the armchair strategists began their usual discussions. Mac McHaffie, our lone Marine, was certain the battle would be a stiff one, and his opinion was backed up by the Army officers aboard. The objective was known to be heavily fortified.

Steady sailing, however, always acts as an antidote to worry. We had at least two and a half weeks ahead of us before we reached the combat area. It was a good time for relaxation.

Before we left Pearl Harbor we had succeeded in purchasing a quantity of musical instruments. Recruiting from the Navy and Army, we were able to find nine men who at some time or other had played in orchestras. There was Ace Parker, rosy-complexioned chief gunner's mate, who took over the drums. Stan Jaskunas, beach party surgeon, squealed out on one of the saxophones. Doc Updergraf of the Army played lead sax, and a youngster from his unit filled in the rest of the section. "Jeep" Williams, boyish-looking fire controlman, played trumpet. Pharmacist's Mate Blackburn and I made up the trombone section. An Army sergeant, formerly a music instructor at Columbia University, was the pianist.

First rehearsals were at best horrible. The crew, a number of whom attended our first meetings, avoided us as much as possible. The boys wanted jive; we were lucky to be able to grind out simple arrangements of "Good Night, Ladies" and "The Star-Spangled Banner."

Two weeks of practice, though, had its results, and the executive officer, impulsive and energetic Dan Hogan, deciding that we were ready for our first concert, proceeded to schedule it.

Though the concert was held in the hot troop mess hall, the turnout was good. Men from the Army and Navy crowded about the orchestra, and made up in applause what we lacked in execution. The program was an amazing one. It included the easiest old numbers we could find, and a few slow modern ones. The jive element was provided by the "Hot Quartet" — Parker, Dunster, Williams, and Updergraf. In addition, we had worked up one specialty arrangement expressly for the executive officer.

Commander Hogan, as soon as he arrived aboard the Doyen in May, had introduced a new phrase in public-address announcements. Each command, repeated twice, was introduced by "Now hear this," and in between the commander interjected, "I say again." Those words — especially "I say again" — irritated the entire ship's personnel. Like true Navy men, we resented any innovations and for want of something better to gripe about, we chose this one for our pet peeve.

At the close of the first group of numbers, Dunster sounded a long roll on his drums. We all broke into the loud caterwauling of the three-ring-circus fanfare. Parker took the floor. "Presenting that latest and greatest of all songs . . . that hit-parade number dedicated to the one and only executive officer of the Dirty D." The words went something like this:

There's a tiresome little phrase we hear at sea

That we never ever heard ashore

And we hope we never hear it anymore . . .

NOW HEAR THIS. NOW HEAR THIS.

If we ever get a chance to get away

You can bet your life we'll find a place to stay

Where we never ever hear a person say . . .

NOW HEAR THIS. NOW HEAR THIS.

I SAY AGAIN!

Commander Hogan, a really good sport, laughed the loudest of anyone.

The Doyen stopped for a few hours at the supply base in the Marshalls. Expecting that we would remain overnight, some of the officers hopped aboard an LCVP for a quick trip to the officers' club. They were due back aboard at 1700. At 1630 the squadron was ordered to get under way.

As we started clearing the channel, we could see a boat from the officers' club headed in our direction. Aboard it were Commander Hogan, Myles Timmins, the chief engineer, Big Joe Donat, the navigator, Archie Alger, the communications officer, Doc Weiner, the dentist, and Chaplain Swinson. It was a good race. We were proceeding at about four knots and the small boat bounced along at twelve. Most of us lined the rails, watching them approach. Rather maliciously we hoped they wouldn't make it; it would make such a good story to tell later on. As the boat came within hailing distance, we could see Commander Hogan pick up his megaphone. Some jokester on the signal bridge, however, beat him to the punch. Drifting down from above us came these words, "Wait for me, Captain. Wait for me. I say again, wait for me." Even Captain McClaughry, standing on the bridge, couldn't suppress a chuckle. It was a sheepish group of officers who were hoisted aboard.

One day later word came that the combat plans had been changed. Why storm a place when it can be by-passed? When it was announced that the Yap operation was canceled, a wave of cheers went up for the high command that could change its plans at the last minute. We had implicit faith in Admiral Nimitz and his commanders, Halsey, Mitscher, Spruance, and Olendorf. Our new destination was an advanced base in the Admiralty Islands.

Among other cargo, we were carrying six war dogs, members of the WAGS. They had been chosen for their size and intelligence and were specially trained for guard duty. Only their trainer dared approach them. It was difficult for us to believe that the friendly looking German shepherds and Scotch collies could be vicious, but we soon learned they were. Long John Barber, walking past one of the dogs, absent-mindedly put out his hand to pat him. The dog leaped forward and only the restraining leash kept him from John's throat.

Sanitation for the animals was difficult. The sawdust-filled box provided for the dogs was anything but pleasant in the hot climate. Space was limited, and the only exercise they could get was on the upper deck aft, where the sun beat steadily down on the metal deck. Most of them developed foot trouble from walking on the hot deck. After three weeks of such conditions they were a forlorn-looking bunch of hounds.

When men live in close quarters and outside recreation is impossible, friction inevitably develops. Such was the case between the Navy crew and the Army passengers. The Army men undoubtedly had sufficient reason for much of their grousing: Water hours were strict (the daily thunder showers had to be used for bathing), the food was monotonous, and the ship provided very little in the way of amusement. The crew, suffering from the same restrictions, was quick to take offense at the Army's complaints. The payoff came one day when the troop adjutant reported to the mess treasurer that the Navy men had more cherries in their fruit salad than the Army!

All signs of trouble disappeared, though, when we anchored in the Admiralty Islands on October 2. With our arrival came the information that we were to take part in the initial invasion of the Philippine Islands; the island of Leyte would be attacked the morning of October 20. There were more important things than cherries to worry about.

12. Leyte

We left the Admiralties on October 13. Although we were experienced veterans by now, we were all worried about this particular invasion. We placed a great deal of faith in Admiral Halsey and his Third Fleet, but we were very aware of the large number of enemy strongholds to be neutralized in the Philippine area.

Within a radius of eight hundred miles there were approximately five hundred Jap airfields. Furthermore, the enemy fleet was still an unknown factor, particularly its submarines, which Intelligence reported were now operating out of the Philippine district. The possibility of floating mine fields was another unpleasant item.

The sailing weather was perfect during the approach. The sea was so calm that we scarcely appeared to be moving and rains were just frequent enough to keep the decks from becoming uncomfortably hot. The temperature remained about ninety degrees day and night.

The morning of the eighteenth the entire convoy was alerted — not because of the detection of enemy aircraft, but to set the condition of watchfulness deemed necessary until after the act of landing was completed. From then until after the invasion, the normal routine of the ship was broken. Gun crews remained at their battle stations in a modified form of general quarters.

The night of the eighteenth passed uneventfully. During the daylight hours of the nineteenth the word was passed for all officers and men to get in as much rest as possible. So, fully clothed, most of our personnel sacked out around the ship — on decks, gun tubs, desks, landing boats, in storerooms, and a few in their bunks. This relaxed condition was to last until nightfall, when additional lookouts would be called to duty. Reveille for the remainder of the ship was to be delayed until 2300.

Needless to say, few of us managed to get much sleep. Encased in a modified form of Mae West life preserver, most of the officers congregated in the upper wardroom. Oddly enough, conversation flourished. The chief topic of discussion was the possibility of the Doyen's return to the States for her promised overhaul.

At 2400, one hour after reveille, all hands adjourned for breakfast — a hearty one of eggs, hotcakes, steak, and cereal. By 0100 the weather decks were lined with anxious personnel.

As at Kiska the weather was an aid to our convoy. A soft rain was falling and a heavy mist obscured the shores of the near-by islands which guarded the entry to Leyte. The only signs of impending battle were the great flashes from the bombardment up ahead.

On schedule, we passed between the outer islands into Leyte Gulf, the second transport to enter. Between then and daylight we were busily engaged in making preparations to debark troops and equipment. Everything proceeded exactly according to schedule. At daybreak we moved into the transport area, steaming to within a mile or so of the beach. Even before the anchor was dropped, the lowering of our boats was begun. We were surprised at the lack of enemy air opposition. Not one attack during the operation thus far. Early on the twentieth we were beginning to believe the Japanese power had been much exaggerated. Ten minutes later we had our first general quarters.

Of all the announcements none packs quite the wallop of "GENERAL QUARTERS . . . GENERAL QUARTERS . . . ALL HANDS MAN YOUR BATTLE STATIONS!" Though you may have heard it fifty times before, the fifty-first still has the freshness of the first. Instinctively you grab your helmet and head for your battle station. Something inside keeps saying, "This may be it . . . this may be it!" The feeling is not so much one of fear as one of intense excitement — the same excitement that you experience on a roller coaster when you approach the first drop.

My battle station happened to be where I could see what was going on. The first glimpse I had of the enemy was through the spots of ack-ack tossed up by our supporting destroyers. The attack was a small one — three high-altitude bombers. Although they undoubtedly released their bombs, none of them lit near enough to be seen. Discouraged by the volume of our defensive fire, the planes swerved away from the harbor area and disappeared. After ten minutes of waiting, all hands were secured from general quarters. The job of unloading continued.

We soon completed the task of transferring to shore the number of troops scheduled to land on the twentieth. The job of ferrying the equipment was not quite so simple. Although the first waves met no opposition, it was some time before the shore installations were sufficiently settled to receive supplies. By dusk we had just begun to make a dent in our holds. Work was scheduled to continue all night.

By 0100 the morning of the twenty-first, the Doyen was pretty well emptied. At 1100 the last of the troops were sent ashore. We had only to wait for the order to leave.

Since we were within a mile of the invasion beach, we had grandstand seats for the show. With binoculars we were able to watch the initial advances inland toward the enemy. One in particular was interesting. The Japs had a pillbox built high on a near-by hill. Like most of their fortifications, this one was constructed to resist shellfire. The pillbox commanded the entire beach and sent a steady stream of lead out toward our landing craft. An order was given to knock out the spot.

The Army tried unsuccessfully for about an hour. We could see their mortar shells sail high through the air to explode almost on the target. But still the box remained. A destroyer then began to lob five-inch shells toward it. The destroyer was ordered to another sector, and a command transport, normally not a shore-bombardment ship, took her place. She pulled into position and began a systematic bombardment with all her artillery. Again we could see the shells. The first of the transport's volleys was effective. The pillbox was split open like a walnut shell. We could see a few men attempting to climb out when the second salvo hit. That was all. What had once been a well-built fortification was now nothing but a white scar on the hillside.

Leyte Gulf is surrounded on all sides by small mountains. This fact makes detection of aircraft quite a problem. Shortly after the bombardment of the pillbox, while the area was enjoying a brief lull, a Jap torpedo plane hopped over a hill, missed us by less than a hundred yards, and swooped down at a near-by cruiser. The torpedo struck home before any of us had a chance to fire. The enemy plane zoomed up into the air and skipped back over the same mountain from which it had come. The whole affair lasted less than two minutes. The warship managed to stay afloat while emergency repairs were made. We last saw her limping out of the harbor, heading presumably for a rear-area repair base. Sixty-nine men were killed and the cruiser was out of action for several months as a result of that surprise attack.

Sunset rolled around again. Smoke generators on all ships were set in operation, and fifteen minutes later the transport area resembled a dense cloud bank. Then we received our sailing orders.

In a way the situation was amusing. In an area of a very few miles there were at least eight hundred ships. Even in clear weather it would have taken great care to avoid collision. Yet here we were, unable to see five feet ahead, maneuvering with the rest of our division to reach the passageway to the open sea.

We had gone less than a hundred yards when a lookout excitedly reported a ship off our port bow bearing toward us on a collision course. Even while his message was being relayed to the bridge, the alert executive officer had seen the shadowy outline of the approaching craft. Time did not permit the use of either radio or blinker. Seizing a megaphone, Commander Hogan bawled out, "Back down! Back down!" We could hear the clanking of the signal bells as the oncoming vessel shifted into emergency reverse. It was almost too late. The bow of the ship, a small patrol craft, slipped steadily closer until it almost nosed against our side. Both ships lay motionless in the water; the megaphone was no longer necessary. "What's the idea?" the commander growled out to the O.O.D. of the other vessel, in a tone that said, "Why the hell don't you watch where you're going?"

The reply was almost apologetic. "There were ships all around us and yours looked the smallest. We stopped as soon as we could."

One of our sister transports, navigated by Dan Minnich (formerly of the Doyen), rammed into a battleship. We heard the radio reports. "Transport damaged in forward peak . . . can proceed immediately." "Battleship reporting . . . blister badly damaged . . . will require repairs." It was a case of David and Goliath.

A week later in an officers' club in the Admiralties, we cornered Minnich and accused him of trying to maneuver an overhaul for his ship. Dan would take no responsibility. The camouflage of the battleship, he said, made her look like two ships. Lookouts on each side had reported objects on each bow. The captain had given the order to go between them. The two objects were the bow and the stern of the battlewagon.

In a few hours we reached deep water. The Pacific had never before looked so good. Except for the men on watch, all of us rolled into our bunks for at least twelve hours of uninterrupted sleep.

13. The Goat and Cabbage Circuit

They asked for the Army
To help at Tulagi,
But Gen'ral MacArthur said "No."
He gave as his reason
It wasn't the season,
Besides there was no USO.
Bless 'em all, bless 'em all,
The young and the short and the tall.
There'll be no promotions
This side of the ocean,
So cheer up, my lads, bless 'em all.

The song was one we had sung for months — a carry-over from the early Solomon Islands' campaign. But now that we were serving under "The Boss," it had ceased to have much meaning. Criticisms by Navy and Marine Corps men of MacArthur's policy of delayed action had been completely wiped out by the skillful execution of the Leyte campaign. His policy of gaining the objective with the least cost in men had proved workable. We were ready to accept the soldier's version of MacArthur: "The best general in the world to fight under."

There were some elements of this new command, however, that we didn't like. Pampered by great stores of Stateside provisions made available to the Central Pacific theater, we were unable to accustom ourselves to the limited diet of the South Pacific.

Dubbed the "Goat and Cabbage Circuit," this area obtained most of its foodstuffs from Australia and New Zealand. There was little variety. Fresh vegetables were limited to cabbage, carrots, apples when in season, and a very few Irish potatoes. Meats consisted of lamb cuts and beef. Vegetable shortening was unheard of; mutton lard was used instead. The prices for these items, established by the joint purchasing boards in Aukland and Sydney, were interesting. Beef sold for thirteen cents a pound; the cabbage cost nineteen cents. Comparable United States prices were twenty-nine cents for beef and three cents for cabbage.

Food has always been the favorite subject of gripes in the armed forces, and our new fare gave us a real opportunity to express ourselves. "What's for chow today?" And always the same answer, "Goat and cabbage . . . even the bread tastes like wool!"

Supply and administrative bases in the South Pacific had been built by the Army and Navy engineers. Construction was always similar. Clearings were whacked out of the dense jungles, and bulldozers pushed out lengthy systems of roadways. Long lines of Quonset huts housed both stores and men. The bases resembled the bleak-looking construction camps built at Boulder Dam and Grand Coulee.

On one of the islands, used jointly by the British and the Americans, we noticed that traffic was routed along the lefthand side of the roads, although most of the vehicles had lefthand drives. With a typical Yankee what-the-hell-goes-on attitude, we asked, "How come?" A representative of the commandant informed us that the United States had occupied the island before the British had arrived, and in order to demonstrate good will, the commandant had ordered his men to learn to drive on the lefthand side of the roads. But when the Australian command arrived, it was learned that the Aussies had been equally courteous; they had been trained to use the righthand lanes! "The only trouble was," our narrator explained, "we got here first."

Most of the bases provided excellent recreational facilities. The bulldozers, after plowing out roads, leveled off spaces for baseball and football. Huge shipments of beer were ordered and distribution centers established.

Intership rivalry, particular between vessels which had operated together for months, was always hot. At each island the officers and men formed softball and touch-football teams. Some of the games were almost bloody. With ball-park fervor, onlookers cheered the favorites and booed the umpires. It would take more than a war to destroy the American love of games.

Shortly after the beginning of the Pacific war the Navy established a system to finance the building of officers' clubs. Money was borrowed from welfare funds, and small buildings were erected on most of the outlying islands. The architecture of the clubs varied from place to place. Quonset huts were used at some islands, and at others, where skilled native labor was available, elaborate structures of bamboo and palm thatching were built.

We visited one of these clubs at the close of the Leyte operation, after an alcoholic drouth that had lasted almost three months. Neatly dressed for the occasion, twenty of us piled into the captain's gig and headed for the beach. The day was hot and the trip long. Ed Bell, a balding, quizzical chap from Virginia, perched himself in the stern sheets and proceeded to extol the virtues of tall, frosty mint juleps. Equally rugged connoisseurs countered with their favorites — zombies, martinis, and boilermakers.

We docked at the club landing. Like a group of boys heading for a fire, we hurried along the crushed-shell path leading to officers' country. The roadway led through a Negro construction camp, which was almost a city. Streets were clearly marked and had obviously been named by the men living there. St. Louis Avenue was the main thoroughfare. Branching from it were Basin Street, Beale Street, and Harlem Street. Basin Street, appropriately enough, led down to the sanitary facilities of the place. Showers and toilets were built out over the water's edge and refuse was dumped directly into the ocean. It was evident that sewage disposal was not a problem.

The officers' club was a pleasant surprise. Located in a small grove of palms, it resembled a movie setting of a South Sea island palace. The long queue of men standing before the door was not such a pleasant sight. Our ship had no corner on the thirst market.

After an hour's wait, we finally crowded up to the bar. Ed Bell, hungry for his julep, placed his order. The bartender looked at him for a moment and then drawled out, "Sorry, sir, but all we got here is beer and whiskey!" Beer and whiskey it was, and there was plenty of both. Life became better with each round of drinks.

At 1700 we headed back to the dock. Linked arm in arm, we could have passed for a delegation at a Legion convention. Commander Hogan led us in a soulful rendition of the "Whiffenpoof Song" (the commander was a Yale man), and we worked from that into "Sweet Adeline" and finally into "Bless 'Em All."

By the time the boat banged against the gangway, a slight wind had come up. Waves whipped against the side of the ship, and footing was anything but secure. The commander was the first to go aboard. As he climbed out onto the side of the boat, reaching uncertainly for the gangway railing, the boat gave a slight lurch. Instead of stepping onto the platform, he plunged feet first into the water. Mac McHaffie dived in after him. The rest of us, slightly befuddled, had all we could do to keep the boat from crushing the men against the side of the ship. A rope was quickly lowered and both officers were hauled aboard. In all respects the afternoon had been a complete success.

One morning we were awakened by a series of shrill cries. "Me-fellow want lop-lop . . . me-fellow want lop-lop." This call came from at least three of the little outrigger canoes that bumped along the side of our ship. What lop-lop was we weren't quite sure, but judging from the heavily laden boats, we guessed that the native pilots were willing to trade.

It was our first close-up glimpse of the primitive Melanesians, and most of us crowded the rails and the gangway. Doc Watkins, in the lead as usual when new experiences were offered, staggered down the gangway under a load of barter goods — old skivvy shirts, trousers, towels, and some brightly colored cloth which he had brought with him from the States. This was language the natives could understand.

One old man, his left leg withered from infantile paralysis, paddled his boat up to the landing platform. From beneath his seat he pulled out a few crudely made spears, a carved paddle, and a bow and arrow. By his motions he indicated that Doc could have his choice, provided he gave all his items in return. Doc was reluctant to make such a trade, and the native stuck to his original offer. Bystanders shouted encouragement to both. After much haggling and many gestures, with neither participant understanding the other, Watkins exchanged his shirts for the paddle and the bow and arrow. In less than five minutes at least fifty skivvy shirts were being dangled over the side. The afterdeck soon began to look like a Zulu armory.

Just off our bow was an island of some size. Through binoculars we could see a series of small native villages built along the shoreline. Naturally we wanted a closer view, so an excursion was planned for 1300.

We landed at the southernmost of the villages. Our boat created quite a sensation among the villagers, and as the prow grated upon the beach we were practically surrounded by boys ranging in age from five to twelve. The older folks, less active but equally curious, formed an interested background.

The houses first attracted our attention. Built of palm and bamboo, they were erected on stilts out over the water. The reason, as Watkins suggested, was to limit possible attack to one direction. From the outside they appeared quite well built and neat. We looked into one of them. It was divided in the middle; one side served as a living room, dining room and kitchen, and the other side was partitioned into sleeping quarters. The women of the house worked and slept in one long room; the small, individual rooms were reserved for the all-important males. What household equipment there was seemed very crude. Bowls were the shells of coconuts; plates were flat sea shells. About ten of each made up the inventory.

We had expected to find a superior group of natives, because, aside from the crippled old man, the outrigger canoes that met our ship had been manned by some very enterprising young boys. But they proved to be the outstanding members of the colony. Probably through their barter they managed to get enough to eat. In any event, they appeared healthy.

The ones that met us ashore were quite different. Little potbellied children with skeletonlike arms and legs, most of them suffering from a variety of skin diseases, confronted us. It was actually nauseating. One little fellow had the underside of his belly covered with open ulcers. Another didn't have an inch of skin that was not peeling. All of them had some type of impetigo. They looked like guinea pigs undergoing some laboratory experiment, not like human beings.

Very few men were to be seen. Those that were visible were, as far as we could tell, doing nothing but sitting. They were the old men of the village, although they were probably not over thirty years old, or at most, forty. With their shriveled faces and their legs covered with tightly stretched parchment, they all seemed to be waiting patiently for death. They were dressed only in loin cloths, with here and there a brightly colored bandana handkerchief. They scarcely bothered to acknowledge our presence.

Not so with the women. At our approach the girls who had come to watch us land ran silently into their huts. The older women, and those with babies at their breasts, stood their ground. Like the men, most of them seemed to be very old, but the fact that many were nursing newborn children belied that impression. They, too, were diseased. I shall never forget the sight of a little baby chewing away at a breast covered with running sores. Doc Gilfillan, watching with a pained expression, remarked, "It's a wonder the kids even survive being born." Stan Gay, who had been extremely anxious to have his picture taken with one of the natives, gradually worked himself to the very rear of our group, staying just as far back as he could.

Perhaps the cause of their condition was malnutrition; perhaps it was due to the introduction of foreign diseases. Anyway, we all felt the greatest pity for them — and also the greatest revulsion. Yet as we stood there, we gradually realized that these people were happy. After the first surprise of our landing, the little groups dispersed and the individuals resumed their tasks — all of them chatting away, laughing, swearing, and some even singing. The little boys dived into their homes to return with all conceivable items of trade. For a few packages of cigarettes I found myself the possessor of five handmade fishing spears.

One old patriarch, dressed in a bizarre costume, managed to rouse himself sufficiently to approach us. For trousers he wore a red and white striped pair of underpants. Around his neck hung a bosun's pipe on a silver chain. His headdress was a baseball cap. Smiling amiably, he saluted. I asked him if he could speak English. His reply was terse. "Talk belong me, he straight; all other kind talk, he cranky. You got kiki?" The word, rhyming with eye-eye, was a new one to us. We showed him a pack of cigarettes; he shook his head. Money brought the same reaction. Finally he rubbed his stomach and made eating motions. Kiki evidently meant food. We finally indicated that we had none, but that we would give him two quarters and two packs of cigarettes for the spears which he held in his hand. He looked at the money for a while, and then stooped over to draw on the ground a circle the size of a half dollar. He stood up, pointed to the drawing, pushed our quarters away, and stolidly folded his arms. He had made his offer. No amount of gestures could convince him that two quarters equaled a fifty-cent piece.

Doctor Watkins asked the old man if he were the chief. The reply was puzzling. "Big fella, he belong house." After repeating it, he pointed to a trail leading slightly inland from the shore.

We walked along the trail the native had indicated. It was narrow and wound through the dense underbrush for almost a quarter of a mile. The trail ended in a clearing, and we saw at the top of a small hill a well-constructed thatched house. A huge black man, dressed in Australian army uniform, stood outside.

The guard had reported our arrival and we were met at the door by an Australian captain. That we were welcome was obvious. White visitors were rare, and this officer lost no time in inviting us into his home.

He told us that he was the island commander and that he had held the post for over a year. Aside from his assistant, a garrulous, rotund warrant officer, the rest of the garrison consisted of a handful of enlisted Australians and a large detachment of native soldiers.

As we drank our host's lukewarm beer — served by a house boy who looked like a cutthroat — he told us about the local customs.

The language spoken on the island was pidgin English diluted with Papuan dialect. Some of his illustrations were amusing. The expression for a wood saw was "Pull 'em he come, push 'em he go; brudder to ax," all spoken rapidly and slurred together. A native song went something like this:

Pies bilong mi i namberwan,

Mi laikim im tasol.

Mi tink long papa, mama tu,

Mi krai long haus blong ol.

Mi wok long pies i longwe tru

Mi stap no gud tasol.

Discipline among the natives was the captain's biggest problem. He had divided the island into two geographical spheres. One, located near the camp, had strict regulations and strict punishments; the other, consisting of the remote island settlements, had few regulations and discipline was lax. If a man in the first group committed murder, he would be shot. If the same crime occurred in the back country, and if it was reported, the offender would be brought to the command base and imprisoned for thirty days. The reasoning was that murder was known to be a serious crime by the near-by natives, but was considered only a healthy form of amusement by the others.

Intertribal disputes were left to the native councils. Their own criminal code was known to all and the island commander hesitated to interfere in its administration. Two weeks before we arrived a married woman had run away with another man. The enraged husband, accompanied by his brothers, followed her and brought her back. She was tried by the local villagers. Her sentence was the usual one for such cases. Her hands were cut off because they had served the other man; her feet were cut off because they had carried her away from her home; a spear was rammed into her genitals because they had been used to entertain the other man. "A bit rough," mused the captain, "but I would have had a mutiny on my hands if I had interfered."

Though the moral code was strict about the conduct of married women, it was lenient about unmarried girls. Laxness was almost encouraged, the idea being that immorality (if it could be called that) would lead to marriage, and marriage was always profitable for the girl's parents.

We asked the captain if he had ever seen any attractive women; the ones we had glimpsed were horrible creatures. He smiled. "You know, they grow less dark each day I'm out here."

When we asked whether the natives had helped in the fight against the Japanese, the answer was emphatically in the affirmative. The Japanese occupation had been unpopular — the troops had appropriated most of the young women — and the men were anxious for revenge. The captain told of a messenger who had reported an enemy encampment about ten miles inland. When he suggested sending an Army unit after them, the messenger indicated that such action would not be necessary. Three days later a half dozen warriors stumbled into the clearing. Skewered to bamboo poles were the heads of thirty-three Jap soldiers. "These natives fight from ambush," the captain explained. "No one can hear them coming, and they can't be seen. They wait for a column of men to come down a trail, then they pick them off with their war arrows."

Curfew on the island was 1700 for all ship-borne personnel. The anopheles mosquito, prevalent on the shore, emerged at sunset. Therefore, to reduce the risk of malaria, all men were required to return to their ships before nightfall.

We stumbled back down the path and climbed into our waiting boat. We had decided to leave any further exploring to the Australians. And they were welcome to the island, too.

14. Christmas — 1944 Style

The anchor chains rattled out and the round, black anchor ball was hoisted to the yardarm. We had just returned from a milk run to Leyte, carrying reinforcement troops, and were again in the Admiralty Islands. The date was November 19. We had encountered more enemy aircraft than on the initial assault landing, but the trip had otherwise been quiet.

As soon as the gangway was lowered, Captain McClaughry left the ship and headed for the command vessel of the squadron. Something important was in the wind — the executive officer intimated as much when he leaned over the rail and wished the skipper luck.

At 1 100 the captain returned to the ship. Fifteen minutes later word was passed for all department heads to meet immediately in his cabin. It was a curious and expectant group that crowded into the room. We thought it likely that a new operation was under way, but we hoped the meeting was for another purpose: the announcement that the often-promised overhaul was at last scheduled.

Captain Mac, clad in his customary brown-and-white-striped seersucker bathrobe, entered the cabin from his bedroom. He was exuberant. "Gentlemen," he began, "you can tell all your men that they will be home in the States in ninety days!" The captain was so pleased over the news that he couldn't stand still. Pacing back and forth in the narrow space, he continued, "I showed the commodore our list of necessary repairs and approved alterations — the long list we compiled a month ago — and told him that something would have to be done about it. The commodore looked over our list, noted that we had been out longer than any of the other ships, and then dictated a report to the amphibious commander. And . . ." the captain paused to give full effect to his next words, "he recommended us for an immediate overhaul!"

Like a group of reporters rushing from a sensational court trial, we burst out into the passageway. The shipboard grapevine was effective and in five minutes all hands had heard the good news.

Stateside! No other word has the same magic effect aboard ship. No hobbies or entertainment can boost morale quite so much as the smallest hope of returning home.

Each officer and each man reacted in some way. Larry Collins, a storekeeper from California, immediately began agitating for body-building exercises. The ship's paper ran a feature story on calisthenics entitled "Can You Still Get Into Your Blues?" More than seventy-five men turned out for the first session.

Archie Alger, the communications officer, ordinarily a cautious, conservative sort of chap, dusted off his dress blues and laboriously polished each brass button. He estimated that our time of arrival in the United States would be December 15.

There were, of course, a few scoffers. Stan Gay and John Barber both insisted that we would not get back until the war was over; they wouldn't believe we were definitely heading for the States until we passed under the Golden Gate Bridge. They refused, however, to back up their opinions with cash.

To combat pessimism Herman Field, the barber, formed a "Believers' Club." There were two good reasons for a large membership in his club: First, most of the men were more than anxious to accept the news, and second, he refused to cut the hair of any nonbeliever.

Optimism ran high. One evening in the upper wardroom Ensign Davenport — a miniature double for Danny Kaye — entertained us with a sample of Stateside life. "Fellows," he began, "when I get back, I'm going straight to the Top of the Mark and get me a few drinks. I'll sit down next to some civilian. When he notices my service ribbons, he'll probably try to start a conversation. I won't pay any attention to him. I'll just keep a sad, tired look on my face . . . and when I pick up my drink, I'll make my hand shake so much that I'll spill a little of the stuff. Pretty soon this civilian will say, 'Tell me, son, how was it out there?' I won't even look at him. I'll just mumble, 'It's too horrible to talk about,' and then get up and limp away. The civilian will watch me go. Then he'll turn back to the bartender and say, 'Must be pretty tough!' 'Must be,' the bartender will agree. They'll both shake their heads, and then the civilian will go back to his drinking. Perfect, huh?"

Nobody could have put quite so much action into the telling as Davie. For the moment he had us all believing that we were actually back at the Mark Hopkins Hotel in San Francisco.

Chaplain Swinson gave us his idea of what to do. "Before I get off the train," he said, "I'm going to take some red and blue indelible pencils and put a fake tattoo on my left arm. I'll draw a spicy little hula gal and put my wife's name under it. I can just see her face when she first sees it!"

"To heck with that noise!" interjected Tom Hawk. "When I get back, I'm going to get as far away from this Navy business as I possibly can. I'll get me a pair of oars, put 'em over my shoulder, and start heading inland. When I get far enough in that someone stops me and says, 'Son, what are those sticks you're carrying?' I'm going to dump 'em on the ground and stake out my claim!"

Chief Pay Clerk Edmonson, our commissary officer, added a word of serious advice. "Whatever else you do, you married fellows make good and sure that your wife knows you're coming. I walked in once after being out for six months. When she saw me standing there in the doorway, she thought I was a ghost and fainted dead away."

And so it went throughout the ship. Everyone was making plans; everyone was dreaming of the wonderful future.

This made it doubly difficult for the captain when, three days later, he was forced to make a different announcement: "This is the captain speaking. The Doyen has been ordered to carry assault troops in a forthcoming operation. Plans for overhaul have had to be postponed until after this next job is finished."

Soon afterward our squadron set sail for the Solomon Islands. Perhaps it was the action incident to being under way that prevented the ship's company from becoming despondent. I prefer to believe that the real cause was the great reserve of hope and confidence most men in the battle zones possess. Whatever the reason, the men took the delay on the chin. As one man expressed it, "This war can't last forever. If our staying out here helps to end it one day sooner, I'm all for it!"

We arrived at Bougainville on December 1. The harbor reminded us very much of the island setting for the movie King Kong. The day was muggy and a mist hung over the shoreline. Dense vegetation spread inland. For three miles the ground was level. Then, as if moulded from clay and placed there by a giant hand, mountains rose steeply upward. To the far right we could see a towering volcano. From its crater came a steady stream of smoke. The effect was one of eerie beauty. Looking at this rugged wilderness, we could easily understand what a difficult task the Army and Marines must have had in wresting it from the Japanese.

It was two weeks before the Army troops and their equipment were loaded. During that period we had plenty of opportunity to go ashore and explore the place.

The war was still going on in the Solomons. In fact, the Allies had attempted to do no more than establish a sizable beachhead and provide sufficient garrison space for the neutralization of the territory. Our control extended only three miles inland. Beyond that there was no guarantee of safety.

We were told that thousands of Japs still remained back in the hills, where they had been isolated for more than eighteen months. Scouts had reported that any semblance of military discipline had disappeared. When their provisions had been consumed, the Japanese, an agricultural people, proceeded to settle down and build small farms. Some of them had enticed native women to join them, and a sizable colonization project had been started. Since these remnants of the Nipponese army offered no great military threat, the Allied policy had been to let them alone. Any advantage gained in destroying them would have been greatly outweighed by the cost in manpower.

Because the mountainous inland area occupied by the Japs was not well suited to farming, some of the more indolent Nips were unable to raise enough to eat. It was not at all unusual for Japanese soldiers to walk into the camp and give themselves up. One officer told of a recreation party some of his men had held. The weather was hot and the soldiers were dressed only in shorts. Time came for dinner. As the men passed along the mess line, it was suddenly discovered that three of the chaps holding out their trays to be served were Japanese.

The same officer was awakened one night by the sound of someone prowling around inside his tent. His flashlight in one hand and a forty-five in the other, he flicked on the light. There at the entrance stood a naked Jap. "These Nips pick the damnedest times to surrender!" the officer commented.

There were times when the foresight of the planners of the war was really appreciated. Such was the case when a representative of the Quartermaster Corps came aboard just as we were about to sail. He asked the number of men the ship was carrying, and then said he would be able to supply us with turkey for Christmas. Until then we had scarcely realized that the holiday season was near. In a region where the temperature stays at a steady 90 degrees, where palm trees comprise most of the larger vegetation, there is very little to indicate the seasons of the year.

The idea of having turkey spurred the men to a few efforts at festivity. A working party volunteered to go ashore on a foraging hunt and returned with bundles of branches that faintly resembled long-needled evergreens. The sprigs were placed under refrigeration.

Fully loaded, we left Bougainville the sixteenth of December and arrived in the Admiralties on the twenty-first. The next four days were spent in the preparations for Christmas. Exchange of gifts was out, of course, so the chaplain arranged to hold a smoker with the Army passengers. Highlights of the program were to be eight boxing matches and music by the Doyen's Hot Quartet. In addition, the bake shop prepared some gooey chocolate pies for a pie-eating contest.

Jack Levenberg, the mailman, contributed his share to the festivities when, on the day before Christmas, he brought aboard forty-six bags of packages from the States! He reported that an LST had been sent especially to provide our task force with its Christmas presents. Though some of the shipping boxes were battered — they had been in the mails for several months — no one minded. The candy, fruit cake, and other gifts could never have been more welcome.

Christmas Day was a complete success, that is, as complete a success as it could be for men who were away from home. Under the tutelage of Charlie Edmonson and Chief Commissary Stewards Walpole and Maloney, the cooks turned out a dinner that would have done credit to Oscar of the Waldorf. The specially printed menu read as follows:

TOMATO JUICE COCKTAIL
SPANISH OLIVES
ROAST YOUNG TURKEY
APPLE & RAISIN DRESSING
CRANBERRY SAUCE GIBLET GRAVY
CANDIED SWEET POTATOES
BUTTERED PEAS
MINCEMEAT PIE ICE CREAM
CANDY MIXED NUTS
LEMONADE
CAFE NOIR
CIGARS CIGARETTES

Following dinner the smoker was held. A boxing ring had been built on the foc'sle, and bleachers were constructed on the forward clipping house and the captain's quarterdeck. At least five hundred men assembled to watch the bouts and smoke the cigars and cigarettes which had been given out.

The Hot Quartet, now consisting of Dunster, Parker, Williams, and Ragsdale, started things off with a few jive numbers. Then came the fights. All of them were fierce while they lasted. We didn't know how the judges graded them, but the results were Navy — 4, Army — 4, and everyone was satisfied. The pie-eating contest also resulted in a tie.

Christmas over, the operational plans were broken out and studied according to the usual routine. We learned that we were to invade Luzon in the Philippines.

15. Up the Slot

In December 1944 our forces had control only of Leyte. The other islands, ribboned with enemy airstrips, were Japanese-held territory. To neutralize them would be impossible. Landing fields, destroyed one day, could be repaired and in operation by the next. Because of Luzon's topography a large-scale landing on its east coast was impractical. The logical invasion points were on the west coast at Manila Harbor, Lingayen Gulf, or Bangui Bay.

Reconnaissance reports showed that the Japs were expecting the assault to be directed at Manila, and in preparation for it they had installed heavy batteries of artillery. Bangui Bay, one of the places where the Japs had landed in 1941, was similarly fortified. The single weak spot was Lingayen Gulf. There were three possible routes to the west coast of Luzon. One was to cross the Sulu Sea through the Sulu Archipelago. This would mean running the ships dangerously close to Borneo. Another was to run the length of the islands on the eastern side, round the northern tip of Luzon, and enter Lingayen Gulf while heading in a southerly direction. This course would bring the convoys within easy range of the land-based planes on Formosa, the Bonins, and the Ryukyus. The third, and the one finally selected by the high command, was a winding passage through Leyte Gulf, the Surigao Straits, and the Mindanao Sea into the Sulu Sea and then north to Luzon. This route would provide the ships with the maximum of air coverage. Navy carrier planes and Army fighters were to form a perimeter of defense; bombing attacks would be carried out against all enemy air bases.

On the morning of January 6 our convoy nosed its way into the narrow Surigao Straits. To our left, within small-arms range, was the mountainous northern edge of Mindanao. It was unnecessary to notify the lookouts to be on the alert; at least twenty pairs of binoculars were trained on the beach. Although we had been warned that Jap PT boats were operating along the coast line, none were seen.

This convoy was the largest with which any of us had yet traveled. Looking out over the water, we could count twenty-five transports, and this was just one group of the many that were to participate. The screen was in proportion and consisted of fifteen destroyers and destroyer escorts. In addition, we were accompanied by three baby aircraft carriers. Despite our evident sea and air power, we couldn't help feeling that this time we were really out on the limb. As one chap expressed it, we were "heading up the slot."

Intelligence reports had not been encouraging. A large enemy task force was reported to be somewhere in near-by waters, and the Japanese were said to be employing a new type of defensive warfare. For some time we had heard of suicide aircraft attacks. Most of them, though, were attributed to individual acts of heroism. It was difficult to believe that any nation would order its pilots, and its planes, to certain destruction. Yet the latest Intelligence communiques had reported that the Japanese were doing just that Tokyo Rose told us of the brave men of the Kamikaze squadrons. (Kamikaze, meaning "divine wind," was a fortuitous gale that had historically saved Japan whenever she was under threat of sea-borne invasion.) These men were pledged to die by diving their planes against American ships. Whether actual squadrons of them existed, we did not know, but one of our patrol boats had picked up the body of one Jap suicide pilot, and it was clothed in a black ceremonial robe.

Shortly after we left the Admiralties, we received two dispatches from the squadron commander. Neither gave us any cause for optimism. The first advised that the operation would be carried out on schedule "if possible." If possible — the words could have a great deal of meaning. The second dispatch dealt with the suicide attacks: "I expect the ships of this squadron to effectively stop any suicide attempts; planes, when diving upon you, present effective targets; fire on them with everything you've got — you can't miss them."

We wondered if the commodore had estimated the length of time a diving plane would be within our gun range. As nearly as we could figure, we would have less than fifteen seconds in which to fire. And only a direct hit would prevent momentum from carrying the plane to its target.

Keith Petty, our disbursing officer, had been relieved by Jim Cason, an officer fresh from the States. Lingayen was Jim's first operation and he didn't quite know what to expect. That afternoon we were sitting in the supply office when — HARRRRUMMMMMM . . . HARRRRUMMMMMM . . . HARRRRUMMMMMM — three planes dived across our fantail, barely twenty-five feet from the surface of the water. Jim jumped from his seat. "What the hell!"

"It's only our own planes," I reassured him. Just then the general alarm sounded. Grabbing our helmets, we rushed out onto the afterdeck.

A Jap twin-engined Betty had been attacked by two of our Corsairs. Realizing that he was lost, the enemy pilot had headed for the convoy hoping to crash his plane into one of our fat transports.

It was like watching a fast-action technicolor movie. Midway between our line of transports and the outside line, the Corsairs caught up with the Betty. We could see the bright red streaks of their tracer shells plow into the Jap plane. Then, as if the Betty had been loaded with TNT, she exploded in midair and fell like a great ball of fire into the sea.

We were still watching, standing there as if paralyzed, when the loudspeaker began booming. The voice of the executive officer almost screamed, "GUN CREWS AND LOOKOUTS . . . DON'T WATCH WHAT'S HAPPENING ON THE PORT SIDE . . . WATCH YOUR OWN SECTOR . . . WATCH YOUR OWN SECTOR."

Action again. Out of the afternoon sun came four enemy fighters. Traveling low and fast, they were within range of our guns. We opened up on them. Each plane appeared to be heading directly at us. Our fire seemed slow and ineffective, although actually machine-gun bullets and shells were pouring forth. This time we were scared; men who had been standing about on the deck disappeared as quickly as if they had been swallowed by the ship. My right leg was trembling. I stepped heavily on it, hoping that no one had noticed. The next few seconds dragged by, each one punctuated by the steady pom, pom of our guns.

The planes passed over us and circled to gain altitude. By this time every ship in the convoy was firing at them. The entire sky was filled with the black bursts of shells. It seemed impossible that any of the planes could avoid being hit. Like great birds, they hovered at ten thousand feet. Then one of them began a long swooping dive at the largest of our transports. We watched it approach through an absolute blanket of lead. Closer and closer it came to its target. Then, at the last moment, the antiaircraft fire took effect. The plane nosed steeply forward and crashed into the ocean, showering the fantail of the ship with blazing gasoline.

Captured Japanese orders had revealed the attack priority attached to our ships. Their planes were to hit carriers first, then the troop transports, although the Betties attacking us had apparently disregarded orders. A second plane began its dive, heading this time for one of the baby carriers. Again the antiaircraft fire was heavy, but the odds were now with the enemy. The plane crashed into the flight deck on the after starboard side. There was a tremendous explosion, and a column of black smoke rose at least two hundred feet into the air. The carrier listed heavily and started to drop back.

The other two Jap planes apparently decided to retreat, for they headed west. As they passed out of the screen of antiaircraft fire, they were immediately hopped on by our fighter escort. The report came in later that both had been shot down.

Behind us in the distance we could still see the smoke rising from the damaged carrier. By sundown she was out of sight. Later that night we heard that she had been abandoned and that one of the destroyers had been ordered to sink her. But her crew must have refused to leave her, for by 0500 emergency repairs had been completed and the carrier was limping along under her own power, still heading for Lingayen Gulf!

The next two days were nightmarish. Although the perimeter screen prevented many of the enemy planes from breaking through, a few did manage to. We were kept almost continuously at general quarters.

As usual there were a few humorous incidents that served to break the tension. Lieutenant Timmins started the rumor that the Doyen had been credited with hitting the plane which had almost crashed into the transport. The gun crews believed him, and without checking with the commanding officer they went ahead and painted a Jap flag on the number four gun tub.

One alert came just at dinnertime. Archie Alger growled out, "They're not going to spoil my steak," and grabbing the hunk of meat in his hand, he padded out into the passageway.

A few die-hards, probably wishing to impress others with their bravery, were reluctant to wear helmets. But after the first raid their policy changed. Not only did they practically sleep in their helmets, but they raised hob with any of their men who didn't follow their example.

Then there was the anti-flash-burn cream. To prevent injury from the intense heat caused by the explosion of bombs and shells, the Navy had developed a thick cream to be used on all exposed skin areas. Our orders were to smear it on our hands and faces whenever an alarm sounded. The result was hilarious. Five hundred men momentarily forgot that a war was going on when they looked at their buddies — all resembling dowagers with mud packs.

We entered Lingayen Gulf at dawn on the ninth. It was the quietest place I have ever seen. The naval bombardment had momentarily ceased and a misty haze hung over the water and the shoreline. Though there were a great many small craft in the water, most of them were at anchor. Except for the steady movement of our own ship, the scene could have been an oil painting. We dropped anchor off the invasion beach and proceeded to unload. Our assault troops were boated in a remarkably short time — twenty-eight minutes, practically a record.

The morning passed uneventfully. Because of the hilly surroundings, we had difficulty in detecting aircraft except by visual means. Our own screen, however, was sufficiently strong to prevent many of the enemy planes from breaking through, although a few did get past to crash-dive some of our units.

Shortly after 1200 word was received for all ships to be on the lookout for any native craft or for floating boxes or other debris. We later learned that a Jap suicide group had commandeered some native canoes, packed them with dynamite, and in the guise of natives brought them alongside two of our transports. As the boats touched the sides of the ships, the Japs set off fuses and dived overboard. The resultant explosions severely damaged the vessels. Another lookout spied a box floating against the current. It was about one hundred yards from his ship and provided a good target, so rather than take any chances, he fired at it. The box disappeared in a great shower of water and smoke. A Jap had apparently tried to swim explosives out to the ship under cover of the box.

News from the beach was encouraging. The first wave had landed and had met no opposition. Beachheads were secured and temporary supply bases established. Only one casualty was reported — a man had been gored by a frightened water buffalo.

By 1500 we were completely unloaded and ready to get under way. Our orders, however, were to stand by until enough ships were emptied to warrant a destroyer screen. We waited for four hours. There were three air raids during that period, but they were all small ones directed at shipping just off the beach.

At 1800 all vessels in the area began to spread a smoke screen. During the three days preceding our arrival, the small mine sweeps, destroyers, and cruisers had been pounded by night attacks. Suicide planes had been reasonably effective, and the smoke screen was used as a defense against both bombs and planes. If the enemy can't see you, he can't hit you. At least, that was our fervent hope.

A smoke screen is quite a sight. Formed from a soupy chemical mixture, it lies on the surface of the water like a dense cloud. It has practically no odor and only mildly irritates the nose and eyes. Its texture is such that wind does not greatly affect it. When properly laid, it forms an excellent protective blanket from the surface as well as from the sky.

Through this artificial fog we were finally ordered to proceed. When we emerged we found ourselves in the company of a convoy almost as strange as the one in which we had left Kiska. There were about fourteen transports supported by three heavy cruisers, two light cruisers, and four destroyers. The cruisers and one of the destroyers were not actually a part of our screen. They had been damaged and were ordered to travel to Leyte with us. Forming a long column on our starboard side, they were a grotesque-looking procession. In the lead was the destroyer. With her mast and bridge shot away, she resembled a huge, squat water bug. Behind her came the larger warships. One in particular, an Australian cruiser, had been hard hit by diving planes, which smashed her stacks and superstructure. The forward stack had been neatly clipped off and the second had been bent almost double. Silhouetted against the sky, it looked like an inverted U. The other vessels seemed relatively intact, but with binoculars we were able to see the blackened and torn spaces that had once been gun turrets.

We received a dispatch the next morning stating that a small Jap task force, probably torpedo boats, had been definitely sighted in the Manila Bay area. Though we thought our air force would keep it bottled up, there was always the chance that it would steam out to intercept us. In preparation for possible trouble, the commodore ordered the two least damaged warships to the port side of the convoy.

That night, just at sunset, the ship's company trampled its way to general quarters. Although I had not heard the alarm, an officer rushing past the supply office shouted the word to me. As I hurried down the ladder to central control, our chief storekeeper — on his way up from the C.P.O. quarters — stopped me and asked what had happened. Before I had time to answer that I didn't know, a bosun's mate burst out with, "That Jap task force is steaming directly toward us. They got four cruisers and ten destroyers!" Just then the loudspeaker announced: "Attention All Hands . . . . General quarters has not been sounded . . . Condition 3-A is still in effect."

The story came out later. Our dentist, Murray Wiener, had been standing on the quarterdeck when he heard the general quarters' bell sound the evening alert on the ship ahead. He had whipped through the upper wardroom, tying on his life jacket as he ran, shouting, "General Quarters . . . General Quarters!" In less than two minutes, with no official order, our ship's company had manned its battle stations. It was a good illustration of what the last week had meant.

On January 12 we pulled into Leyte Harbor. Less than two months before we had been glad to leave Leyte; now we were thankful to return. We were nerve tired and physically exhausted — and we were convinced that there would never be another run like that to Lingayen.

16. Stopover at Guam

The war in the Pacific was moving rapidly. In less than twelve months our forces had swept across more than forty-five hundred miles of enemy territory. The Philippines were now ours except for mopping-up activities, and from Guam and Saipan, daily hordes of sleek B-29's were heading out over Tokyo.

Future strategy was clear. We had both air and sea supremacy; we could hit where we pleased and when we pleased. First we would soften the Japanese homeland itself. Perhaps this would cause the enemy to surrender. If it didn't, an invasion would follow. If resistance was directed from China and Manchuria, troops would enter there.

To accomplish this next phase, certain new advanced bases had to be established. Running southward from the lower tip of Japan are two island chains — the Ryukyus to the westward and the Volcanos to the east. Since both had been heavily fortified by the Japs, they now served as impediments to our bombing raids. But once they were in our hands, they would accomplish three vital purposes: They would effectively isolate Japan from the China Sea; they would provide bases for our own bombers and fighter-support planes; and they would provide excellent areas from which to launch our invasion attacks. It was toward these island chains that the high command was now looking.

While the run to Lingayen was still fresh in our minds, we were notified that a new assault had been scheduled. The goal was to be the tiny Volcano island of Iwo Jima — located just 650 miles south of Tokyo.

We rendezvoused at Ulithe, an advanced fleet base. With us was a great aggregation of sea power. For fifteen miles the water was covered with the hulls of battleships, cruisers, aircraft carriers, destroyers, and fleet auxiliaries. The heavier units were to leave before us; their job was to do the initial softening up of Iwo, as well as to attack the actual Japanese coast line. The air wing was scheduled to hit at the enemy airfields in the Bonins, the Ryukyus, and in Japan proper. We would depend upon the air force, too, to provide us with an effective screen. Amphibious landings in stormy weather are bad enough (Iwo was scheduled for mid-February) without the additional hazard of air raids.

On February 6 we left the Carolines and steamed northward to Guam. Guam was already established as a major supply base, and we were to stop off there for fuel and provisions. Since the average February temperature in the Volcanos is 50 degrees, we were also required to take on a complete stock of winter clothing.

The delay gave us a chance to spend a little time ashore. It was actually a thrill to set foot again on United States soil — particularly since we had taken part in the invasion which had freed it.

In appearance Guam was not unlike Saipan. It was a beautiful island. Though mountainous, there was much land suitable for farming. The level country was a patchwork of rice paddies and truck gardens; the hillsides were covered with many varieties of utility timber.

About nine miles to the left of the main harbor was the capital city of Agana. A copy of the National Geographic had pictured it as a colorful Spanish-style settlement, but when we reached it, we found only a tumbled mass of ruins. During the initial assault, the Japanese had made a garrison of the city, and the natives fled to the hills. Agana was then declared a proper target and was pounded by both naval and ground artillery.

There is nothing, I believe, quite so ghostly or macabre as a city desolated by war. On one side of a narrow little street stood a jagged section of wall. There was only enough left to indicate that at one time a fine house had stood there. Under a pile of rubble I could see a few children's toys — a rag doll and the wheel from a baby buggy. The doll was pinned between two stones. Its head was free, bobbing up and down in the wind. Another home was sliced slantwise from top to bottom. Part of two stories still remained. But that was unusual. There was block after block of completely gutted and battered buildings. It was as if the town had undergone a tremendous earthquake and had then been thoroughly crushed under the wheels of a gigantic steam roller. The churchyard silence of the place was broken only by the rumble of our trucks as they passed through. Here and there we could see little groups of natives picking through the charred piles of wood and clay that had once been their homes.

We stopped off at the civil command base, which had been established in temporary quarters in the heart of the town. The project then under way was to find suitable living quarters for the natives and to set in operation a plan that would ensure the eventual rebuilding of Agana.

It is difficult to avoid referring to the inhabitants of Guam as natives. Actually they are citizens of the United States. Yet in color and facial characteristics they resemble a half-caste mixture of Mexican and Japanese. An extremely friendly people, they greeted us with smiles and snappy salutes. Some of the women were beautiful, even by our standards. The Navy had used Guam as an operational base for a great many years, and old-timers aboard ship said that intermarriage had been common.

One afternoon we took a jeep and bounced over a newly carved road to the Guam airbase. Located on a plateau up in the hills, it was a masterpiece of American engineering. How long or wide it was I can only estimate, but it must have been at least two miles from one end to the other. The surface of the field was concrete and a composition substance resembling tarvia. We stopped at the security office and obtained permission to explore the place.

Our first interest was the B-29's. Like great gulls, hundreds of them were lined up along the runways. Some had just returned from Tokyo; others were preparing for the next trip. There were even more B-24's. Some of them had more than ninety missions recorded on their shiny noses. Each sported at least one life-sized drawing of a pin-up girl and each was named for some Stateside miss. There were "Mistress Mary," "Lulu Belle," "Sweet Sue," "Angel Face," "Lil Audrey." The one exception, of historic interest to us, was "Tokyo Rose." She had been the first land-based plane to fly over the capital city of Japan.

Wherever the armed forces go, entertainment goes with them. One evening I was invited to attend the "Guam Swing-Shift Show." Staged and presented by a native (Mrs. Johnson by name!), the program was held in the open-air theater behind the supply depot. The group, composed of local talent, attempted to imitate the movie versions of New York stage productions. Three little girls, none of them over fifteen years old, labeled themselves the Guamettes and did a brief dance routine. From the smiles on their chubby faces, it was evident that they enjoyed it as much as the audience did. The girls didn't dance well, nor did they dance in unison, but for many of us it was the first live entertainment we had seen in over a year. One number was particularly good. Joaquin Manibusan, a slender Spanish-looking chap whose tenor voice resembled John McCormack's, sang several native songs. We later learned that he was the Frank Sinatra of the Guam radio station.

What drew the greatest applause, though, was a hula dance by Marion Johnson. The South Pacific hula barely resembles the suggestive version so often seen in nightclubs in the United States. The real hula is a slow, weavingly graceful dance, with great emphasis on the movements of the arms and hands. Each dance tells a story and each motion is a part of that story.

After the program the cast was invited to dinner in the officers' mess hall. Judging from the gusto with which they attacked the buffet supper, we reasoned that food had been the primary reason for their gesture at entertaining us.

As soon as the meal was completed, a phonograph was started and some of the men began dancing with the girls. One of the men, Lieutenant McCrae, had told me earlier in the day that his policy was, "Anything for the fleet." Remembering the phrase, I approached him; he grudgingly allowed me to cut in.

I had not been on a dance floor for more than a year, and my heavy beach-party shoes didn't improve the situation. Furthermore, my partner was short and barely came above my waist. We plodded about for a few minutes. Rather embarrassed, I tried to start a conversation. "Do you like to dance?" was the best I could manage. Though her reply was "Yes," her tone added, "but not with you, you clumsy ape." I gladly relinquished her to McCrae.

We left Guam a few days later and headed north. With each passing day we could feel the temperature change. It was actually cold when we approached Iwo Jima; a storm was brewing and the waves were running high. The date was February 19.

17. Iwo Jima: The Goal

A cold rain was falling when we entered the transport area. Gun and deck watch crews were standing like solitary penguins, water dripping steadily from their rain gear. In the foggy distance, about three miles off our port bow, lay the island of Iwo Jima.

Iwo was a small island — only nine thousand yards long, and at its widest point, barely four thousand yards across — and it resembled a shroud-covered body. Mount Suribachi, an extinct volcano, rose steeply at the southern point. From the base of the mountain northward the ground sloped gradually up until it met the jagged, square cliffs of the north end. Aerial reconnaissance photos showed that from the air Iwo Jima looked like a miniature South America.

Unlike Lingayen Gulf, this was not a quiet spot. It had been blasted for eighty days, and it seemed that every unit of the fleet was joining in the present bombardment. At one time or another, practically every battleship in the Pacific had been there throwing in tons and tons of shells at point-blank range. Some came in so close that they had to pull out to sea to give drop to the trajectory of the fire. They were not aiming to hit within a dispersal area of twenty-five yards; they were firing to hit the exact target.

Add to this the cruisers, the destroyers, and the rocket-firing gunboats. Because of the lack of recoil from rockets, anything from a rowboat on up could fire them, and practically everything did. Then there were the small craft equipped as mortar-firing boats, some carrying heavy machine guns. All these craft would slide up close to the coast and blast away angrily at individual Jap positions that had been spotted. One boat in particular fired hundreds and hundreds of rounds at 200-yard range. It was done with such seeming viciousness that we felt the skipper of the boat must have some private grudge against the defenders.

The sky was almost black with our carrier planes. They kept coming from the carriers at sea in an unending stream. Fighters with bombs and rockets made run after run. Dive-bombers by the score, hour after hour, concentrated on each individual strong point.

A few of our planes got shot down. Sometimes they would get too interested in observing the fall of a bomb and would fly over a hornet's nest themselves. One TBF was being fired on heavily. While we watched, a thin wisp of smoke began drifting astern . . . the plane became a torrent of black billows . . . the whole underside burst into flame. The plane headed out to sea, still floating lazily, but unable to gain enough altitude to allow a successful parachute jump by the crew. The flames were enveloping the plane, and though still flying gracefully it drifted lower and lower. We could sense the struggle that must be going on within the ship. A plane already aflame does not give the fliers a chance when it hits the sea. Finally one man managed to throw himself clear of the blazing wreck. We watched him grapple with his chute. It did not open, and he hurtled into the water a few moments before his plane hit. All that remained was a black swirl of smoke.

We looked at each other and tried to grasp the fact that a moment ago there had been two men alive in that plane — two men, thinking and feeling. Now there was nothing. It was like watching a spectacular play one second and having the curtain drop the next. It was unreal and yet we knew it had happened.

Into this maelstrom of lead we sent the first wave of troops. The wind had died down, fortunately, but the water was still rough. The beach was slightly sloping, with a surf action that threw up seven to ten-foot waves. It was the toughest sort of a landing to make, for once a boat turned sideways it would be swamped immediately. The skill of experienced coxswains, however, got most of the boats onto the beaches in excellent order. It was miraculous that there were so few landing casualties.

Then it began! Returning boat crews told of the hell of mortar and artillery fire that broke loose. From previously prepared positions the Japs had fire charts for every square yard of the beachhead areas. They had all the high ground, as well as the perfect observation given by Mount Suribachi. We asked one boy what it was like. In a dull, matter-of-fact voice he in turn asked us, "Did you ever try to dodge the drops of rain in a thundershower?"

From the beach line up to the central plateau was a distance of eight hundred yards, and the ground rose sharply. Had not the naval gunfire, rockets, and planes kept them under cover, the Japs could have lain at the crest of the hill and with small-arms and machine-gun fire ended the invasion attempt right there.

We began receiving casualties that afternoon. From their stories we pieced together a picture that promised to make Saipan look like a minor skirmish.

The continent of Europe has hundreds of miles of coast line that must be defended from an invasion. Necessarily, the beach defenses will be spread relatively thin. The defense of a coast line does not contemplate preventing landings; it plans to make the landings as difficult and as lengthy as possible. The time thus gained is used to shift mobile reserves to a point where they can successfully attack. This was the way it went in France and in Leyte, and would have gone in Luzon if the Japs had had any mobility of action. But when you attack Tarawa, you attack Tarawa; when you attack Iwo Jima, you attack Iwo Jima. That is all there is to it. The garrison forces have only so many yards of beach that can be assaulted, and they proceed to build adequate defenses. The Japs had years to prepare for the battle of Iwo Jima.

The principal characteristic of the island was a complicated system of caves. To picture them, think of a large and intricate spider web, and then imagine it underground beneath a layer of five to ten feet of rock. The Japs could go literally anywhere and everywhere throughout that island without ever seeing daylight. Every cave on the side of a hill, on the rugged, sheer slopes of Suribachi, inside the volcano crater itself, was connected with some other cave. Each pillbox or strong point on the relatively level ground could be reached by an underground shaft that led to one or more similar points.

One blockhouse, its concrete walls four feet thick, could be reached by eight different tunnels leading into it like the spokes of a wheel, and each tunnel led to some other blockhouse, pillbox, underground kitchen, or munitions dump.

In one gigantic cavern linked to any number of passageways, there was discovered a distillation unit capable of making one hundred thousand gallons of fresh water a day. Fifteen thousand Japs could be supplied comfortably on the production of that one unit; forty-five thousand could be supported by it in an emergency.

Many of the caves had steel doors and railway tracks. The doors would flash open for an instant, an artillery piece would roll out, be fired at a prearranged setting, and then roll back again, all in a matter of seconds.

Picture what all this meant in making an advance. Pillboxes had to be knocked out before an assault could be made past them. A detail of men had to be ordered to neutralize them. A lieutenant colonel of the Third Marines, a casualty, described the method he had used. "I sent twelve men forward while the rest of us kept them covered with a barrage of mortar and artillery fire. We tried to aim at the gun slots in the box. But by the time the men reached the point where they could effectively place their dynamite charges, more than half of them had been wounded or killed. Once the blasts went off, the rest of us crawled forward and stuck our flame-throwers in the slits. We tossed in a few grenades for good measure. We thought the job was done. But after we had pushed ahead, some Japs re-entered from an underground tunnel and fired on us from the rear. I've decided that the only sure method of knocking out a pillbox is either to blast shut all the connecting passageways or to post a permanent guard."

Few of the casualties had seen any Jap soldiers, either dead or alive. This puzzled them until they learned about the complex system of tunnels. Whenever a pillbox was knocked out, the enemy dead and wounded would be dragged back to some other point. One nineteen-year-old veteran, who came aboard with dozens of painful but not fatal shrapnel wounds, had gone into a knocked-out box to make sure that no one was left in it. He had just about completed his search when he and his buddy heard someone coming down a large, dark tunnel leading into the box. As they aimed their rifles, they heard something strike the ground at their feet. The fearful buzzing noise of a grenade began.

Doctor Gilfillan asked the boy, "What did you do then?"

"We started to git out of there," he replied.

"Then what?"

The answer came in a dry voice, tinged with chagrin. "We didn't git fast enough!"

It was only D-day plus one when General Holland Smith announced that the battle of Iwo Jima was the bloodiest, most bitter fight in Marine Corps history.

For the next two days we lay in near the shore. Aside from the overworked hospital ships, we were one of the few heavy ships receiving casualties. On the night of D-day plus three word was received that a new load of wounded was ready for transfer. The men were resting in temporary dressing stations set up on four LST hospital auxiliaries located about three hundred yards off the shore. I asked permission to ride along in one of the boats. The captain consented, but added, "Be careful. There's no reason in God's world for a supply officer to get killed."

Tom Hawk was assigned as boat officer, and he and I climbed atop one of the davits and lowered ourselves into a boat. We were on a level with the top deck of the ship, and could get a good view of the coast line.

Though the night was cloudy, the brilliant glare of parachute flares outlined the island. The yellowish white lights were ours; the red lights were those of the Japanese. Five miles to the left, silhouetted against the sky, was Mount Suribachi. According to our instructions, the LST's were lying to off its base.

The davit lines whirred, lowering the boat to the water. We knew that the trip ahead of us would be long, and both of us wore fur-lined jackets, life belts, forty-fives, and battle helmets. As we pulled away from the ship, Commander Hogan shouted down that he would maintain a signal for us on the yardarm. "Watch for red over white over red. We'll show it for one minute every five minutes."

The water around Iwo Jima was not suited to small craft. A thousand feet away and our ship had almost disappeared from view. The mountainous waves tossed us like a chip of wood from crest to valley until it was all the coxswain could do to hold a steady course.

As we drew nearer the beach, we could get an occasional glimpse of the ground fighting. Even from a distance of several miles, we could hear the horrendous roar of the rockets. The only comparable sound would be that of a fast freight passing directly over you. A battleship, lying just beyond the horizon, was lobbing shells over us. And there is no more terrifying noise than the shriek of a sixteen-inch shell.

We had some difficulty in locating our LST. Each control vessel we asked would direct us farther in toward the shoreline. But finally we found our assigned ship barely one hundred yards from the base of Suribachi.

There were several boats ahead of us, bringing more casualties from the beach. The stretchers were placed on a pontoon barge alongside the LST and a sling hoisted them aboard. We were finally ordered to tie up. Tom leaped out onto the raft and approached the officer in charge of the loading and unloading. A moment later I heard him cry out in surprise. When I looked up, he and the other officer were almost dancing together. Tom dragged his companion over to the boat. "Larry," he said, "meet my cousin Jim. He's the Doc on this tub!"

We could carry six stretcher cases and twelve ambulatories. While we waited for them to be lowered from the ship's deck, Jim Hawk gave us his version of the fight. He had never before seen so many casualties. In three days his ship alone had handled more than 1500. They came aboard in an endless stream; as fast as they could be checked and classified, they were transferred to some other ship. There was not sufficient time to treat each patient thoroughly, and to make matters worse, most of the wounds were filled with the finely granulated volcanic ash of the island. All that could be done was to administer morphine and hope that other ships would send aid.

While we talked, the mountain, looming directly above us, was suddenly bathed in light. An attack was commencing and a cruiser had turned her searchlight on Suribachi. High up near the top, we could see the entrance to a deep cave. Though it had been blasted time and again, it was still filled with enemy soldiers. Jim and Tom had the only available binoculars and they told me what happened next. Two Nips attempted to climb out of the cave and up the steep wall, but lookouts on the cruiser saw them and a solid line of tracer shells whipped directly into them. By the time Tom relinquished his glasses, all I could see was a grayish scar on the side of the rock.

Fifteen minutes later we loaded our casualties into the boat and shoved off. The trip back to the ship was hellish. The water seemed rougher than before, and I could almost see the casualties getting seasick. One chap, his arms bandaged, was seated next to me on the stern sheets. His face was a sickly green and he was doing his best to keep from vomiting. Conversation sometimes helps at a time like that, so I asked him the usual question, "Where you from?"

"Iowa, up near the Minnesota border."

"That wouldn't be anywhere near Luverne, would it?" I asked, Luverne being my home town.

"God, yes — just twelve miles from there!"

In a few minutes he had given me his name, Bob Smith. I had heard it before; a relative of his had owned a bakery in Luverne. It wasn't long before we had named other mutual friends: Woody Hetlund, star football player in high school and later at Morningside College in Sioux City, and Chet Dunn, a farm boy, now somewhere on Luzon. Smith was feeling much better, but the other casualties were not.

We seemed to have been riding for hours. Since we were no longer heading into the light from the beach, visibility was extremely poor.

Tom and I checked bearings. We had been pointing toward the sea for two hours, and it had taken us only ninety minutes to make the trip in.

Either we were lost or the Doyen had changed her berth. There were no large ships in sight; nowhere could we see a mast carrying lights red over white over red. Suddenly a ship loomed out of the darkness. It was under way, and we speeded up to run alongside it.

Tom took the megaphone and roared, "WHERE ... IS . . . THE . . . DOYEN?" After five minutes, a thin voice filtered down, "We . . . don't . . . know!"

Again we headed out to sea. By this time the situation was getting serious. The stretcher cases had been tossed about unmercifully and the ever-increasing waves threatened to swamp us. We were almost ready to turn back when Tom spied the silhouette of the Doyen.

Twenty minutes later we bumped along her side. Slings were lowered and the casualties were taken aboard. "Where in hell have you been!" I snapped at the first lieutenant as I finally crawled over the railing.

"You can consider yourself damn lucky," he replied. "An hour after you left, we got orders to retire farther out to sea for the night. The captain really stuck his neck out coming in even this close."

18. Iwo Jima: The Price

It was D-day plus eight, and for the first time in more than a week there was the sound of laughter in the upper wardroom. Ensign "Bones" Rowan, an extremely tall, slender, anaemic-looking chap, had been sent to a hospital ship to obtain a supply of whole blood. Timmins was telling us about Bones' reception on the other ship. "Bones crawls up on the deck. It's littered with stretchers, patients, doctors, corpsmen, and just about everything. He goes up to the nearest doctor and says, 'I want some blood.' Before he has time to explain, the Doc takes one look at him, throws him down on the deck, and pumps two transfusions into him!"

Casualties were still coming aboard. Since we had landed almost all our troops, we had sufficient space for hospitalization. The doctors were working night and day. Occasionally they would find time for a few hours of rest, but those times were so infrequent that it was a wonder to the rest of us that they could keep going. Our regular staff, Doctors Gilfillan, Kelly, Watkins, and Jaskunas, had been increased by two younger men from the base hospital at Guam. It was the first time, however, that either Doctor Wier or Doctor Gorsuch had handled combat casualties.

Every time a boatload of wounded approached the ship, the loudspeaker announced: "Second Division and medical department stand by to receive casualties." The boat would bump alongside the ship. To lift the casualties aboard, a davit had been constructed that would swing clear of the side of the ship. From it dangled a special set of rigging that provided four loops of line to fit over the handles of a stretcher. A hand-operated block and tackle was used to hoist the stretchers from the boat to the ship's deck. There were four steadying lines. Two, on the outboard side of the stretcher, were let down to the man in the boat. A strain was taken on those two lines to prevent the stretchers from banging into the side of the ship on the way up. The other two lines, on the inboard side, kept the stretchers from swinging too far out.

We had several men who were experts in handling this operation, and they were always put into the casualty boat when it first came alongside. The difficulty was that the boats would bounce up and down in the heavy swells, and if a strain was taken on the rigging with a stretcher still on the deck of the boat, the rise and fall of the sea would give the wounded man a terrific jolting. The trick was to lift the stretcher clear of the deck and provide a sort of "knee action" by raising and lowering the stretcher as the sea rose and fell.

When all was secure, the men on the ship would take a heavy strain and lift the stretchers clear. The fact that the stretchers were four feet above the bottom of the boat before the lifting started provided a margin of safety should the boat suddenly ride up on a swell. Luckily we never had an accident in bringing the casualties aboard. In fact, none were even badly jolted.

For most of us, unless our ship was hit and our men wounded, there was little reality to war except for the casualties we brought aboard. Everything else was a kaleidoscopic, technicolor, supercolossal theatrical production.

But when we looked down and saw a dozen stretchers on which were lying twelve broken, bloody men, then the war became real, horribly so. It was not so much that they were torn and dying; it was that three or four days ago they had been men who could hike thirty miles a day at double time, and after a few hours' rest do it over again. They had been our best. Always there was the look in their eyes — numbed, unseeing, unfeeling — that communicated the horror enemy mortar fire must be, and how it must seem to look about you and find that most of your platoon are gone.

Even the most terrific naval actions of this war have involved firing periods that could be counted in minutes. Either a ship is torpedoed or it isn't; either you sink their cruiser or they sink yours; either a dive-bomber hits you or it doesn't. In any event, it is all over in a short time; either you are safe or you are dead. But the men we received aboard as casualties had experienced constant and deadly enemy fire for periods lasting anywhere from two hours to eight days. Nothing in the European theater could have compared with Iwo Jima. Here there were no prepared positions to fall back to, no chance for any relief.

Once the casualties were brought aboard, they were taken to the troop mess hall where a central sorting station had been established. They were immediately x-rayed, and plasma and whole blood were poured into them. Men came aboard ship grievously wounded, in extreme shock, and scarcely breathing. As soon as their stretchers were placed on the sorting station deck, corpsmen would start pumping plasma into them. Some men who otherwise would not have lived another hour were talking and joking with us a few minutes later. Color returned to their faces, they came out of shock, and their normal respiration began. As we watched the administration of plasma, we could actually see life begin to flow back into their bodies.

Many of the men brought aboard suffered from "shell shock," or "combat fatigue," as it is called in this war. But call it what you like, we did not have to be psychiatrists to realize that the human mind can look at one scene just so long, can absorb meaning and reality to just a certain point. With these men that point had been passed. Their minds had refused to accept the pictures which their senses presented; it was as if a screen had been placed between them and reality. Some blabbered idiotically; others just sat quietly, saying nothing, staring straight ahead. Some would never be rational beings again.

A few of the soldiers came back without a wound on their bodies or a strain to their minds. They were just so utterly exhausted that every muscle had stopped functioning. They were too tired to stand, to move their mouths or their stomach muscles, or to perform normal body functions. We put them to sleep for three or four days. After that a day or so in the sun made them as good as new. These men volunteered to go back to their units.

Worst of all were the shrapnel and mortar wounds. Shrapnel penetrates men's bodies, with varying seriousness, from the top of their skulls to the base of their feet. If it enters the stomach, the doctors have a "belly job" that takes an operating period of two to four hours. The mortality rate is highest for this type of wound, and operations must be performed immediately. Other casualties have to wait.

The control medical section on the beach attempted to distribute the work load evenly among all the transports. But sometimes, when there were few heavy ships in the anchorage, the Doyen had to take almost all the casualties. Even though this meant that some had to wait hours for an operation, they were still better off on board ship than they would have been on the beaches. The second they came aboard they got plasma, whole blood, and penicillin or sulfa compound — to prevent their growing worse until the doctors could get to them.

There were many human interest stories. One youngster began talking under the anesthetic while his leg was being amputated. Apparently he was picturing his return home and the horror he would see in his mother's eyes. His words were, "I didn't do much, Mom, only my job."

We had a motor machinist's mate named Altman on board. His brother was with the Third Marines, in the thick of the fight. As the casualty lists mounted, Altman became more and more worried. On D-day plus twelve an LSM came alongside loaded with casualties. Among them was his brother. Altman practically flew to him and stayed by his side all that night and the next day. There were tears in both brothers' eyes when the stretcher was brought aboard. We knew that deep down inside they had never expected to see each other again.

Captain Anderson commanded one of the other transports in our squadron. His son, who had been in one of the assault battalions, was brought aboard horribly and hopelessly mangled. He had been doped with morphine and was not in too much pain. The boy called for his father, and when he arrived, said, "Dad, I sure hope you've got some good doctors aboard." He died shortly afterward, and his father took him ashore and buried him in the Marine cemetery on Iwo Jima.

There was one Marine captain whom we all admired. When he was brought aboard, he was not expected to live, but he fought for his own life as valiantly as he had attacked the enemy (he had received the Navy Cross at Saipan). A week later he had one of our men write a letter for him. It read: "Dearest, here's the score. My right leg is gone and my left leg is useless. Otherwise, I'll be O.K. What do you want to do?" We had no doubts as to what the reply would be.

Another man did not have the aggressive spirit of the captain. He had been in four major operations and was the last soldier left from his original company. The chaplain talked to him one night, shortly after the doctors had said he would live. "Chaplain," he said, "my number is up. I just know I'm going to die." By morning he was dead.

Another casualty regained consciousness while he was being prepared for the operating table. Looking up, he saw Chaplain Swinson about to remove his wrist watch. In a feeble voice he objected. "You don't need my watch . . . you've got a watch."

Swinson reassured him. "Don't worry, son, you're not dying. I'm the chaplain. I'll keep your watch safe for you." The boy grinned and closed his eyes.

Donald Yent, our Chinese American fountain operator, took almost personal care of the sick wards. Each day he loaded a box with cups of ice cream and carried it around from patient to patient. It was more help than many of us were able to give.

19. A Letter Home

Though we all took a personal interest in the casualties, the responsibility for them, of course, belonged to our doctors. Robert Watkins wrote a letter home in which he described his own reactions. With his permission, it is included here.

March 11, 1945

Dear Folks,

Since by now you have probably received the impression from my letters that my part in this war is devoted largely to sightseeing, exploring South Sea islands, and surfing, I shall devote this to my more serious activities. I want you to see the battle as I see it; not as a news reporter would see medical personnel caring for war casualties, but as I personally am conscious of these scenes. ... I'll give you a few hours of my part in several weeks of fighting.

Since I cannot describe the picture completely if I try to spare your civilian sensibilities, I shall leave a very minimum to your imaginations. If your stomachs are queasy, stop here.

In the gray dawn we drew into the battle area, just as the first assault waves were hitting the beach. The air and surface of the sea trembled with the vibrations of the cannonading, the rocket explosions, the dive-bombing, the explosions of Jap shore ammunition dumps, the popping roar of small boat engines. The gently sloping sides of the rugged rocky island that was our target blazed with fire. Fountains of fire wove their way up into the air toward our dive-bombers as the Japs tried to interrupt their downward swoops. Falling shells raised flowery splashes from the surface of the sea. Tracer shells ricocheted by like little fireflies skimming the waves. This continued for hours during our approach into the offshore area selected for the unloading. I sat on deck, nursing my nervous tension, trying to enjoy the sunrise and the welcome change of a cold wind blowing against my face, and conserving my strength for the days of exertion that were to come.

During the days and nights that followed, sometimes we were so close to shore that we could see the infantry and tanks fighting, almost as though they were in our backyards. On others we were far out in the ocean. Some days were clear and lovely; on others the chill wind and fog whipped across the scudding whitecaps, raising waves that almost wrecked our landing boats. Some days the sun shone and I did not know it. Some nights the moon was bright, but not for me. Some sunrises I watched through the porthole as I washed the blood of the night's work from my hands and clothes. Sometimes I got to bed by midday. Sometimes not at all.

Since we were not scheduled to receive casualties in the early parts of the engagement, we laid offshore some distance to wait our turn. However, along came a Higgins boat whose coxswain had lost his way looking for the ship to which his casualties were assigned. Since many of them were seriously wounded, we took them alongside, hoisted the litters over the rail, and carried them into the troops' mess hall (dining room to you landlubbers), from which the tables had been removed and laid in regular rows upon the deck. Here I saw the casualties for the first time. Occasionally small numbers, usually forty or more at a time, were brought in from the main deck by volunteer litter-bearers from our crew.

A thousand impressions of the pandemonium in the mess hall flit through my mind. Corpsmen not assigned elsewhere are setting up portable stands and starting plasma and blood running into the veins of those in serious shock. One or two circulate about, recording names, units, ratings, relatives to be notified, and so on, before the patients are moved to compartments, operating rooms, the chaplain's compartment, and other distant portions of the ship. Litter-bearers are in constant motion, moving the injured for x-rays, cutting off grimed clothing and dirt, lighting cigarettes, getting drinks of water, and otherwise trying to make the men more comfortable. Troops and crew members off duty stand at one end of the hall, giving us a hand when called upon.

Ambulatory wounded, combat-fatigues, mental patients, x-rayed men, men on duty going to and from their stations, men eating, men stationed with the telephones, corpsmen, ship's officers, passengers — all are passing to and from the four corridors and three ladders that open on this mess hall. Bloody dressings, empty plasma and blood-transfusion bottles, discarded and fouled clothing and splints gather in corners. Men squat by the litters, steadying the arms of casualties receiving intravenous fluids, washing and shaving dirty limbs and bodies in preparation for operations. Doctors stand around waiting for patients to be prepared or for their condition to be sufficiently improved to permit transfer to the operating room, directing or aiding with the administration of blood and plasma, inspecting wounds and x-rays, consulting with each other about decisions for treatment. A constant interchange of humanity flows in and out of the space. New casualties on foot, on litters, hobbling, half-carried, move in, further crowding us until there is hardly six inches between the long rows of litters.

Battle-fatigue patients and those with minor wounds or wounds that can wait until the more serious cases have been attended to are being taken to bunks in distant compartments of the ship, after they have been registered and given clinical charts. Patients are carried by litter down the corridor to the operating room on the deck below, or up the steel ladder to the auxiliary operating room in the ship's officers' wardroom on the deck above. . . . Sometimes as the litter tilts to ascend the ladder, a cascade of blood drools to the deck from the pools that have gathered under the patients. At one side of the room the x-ray machine has been set up, and to it are carried a jerky stream of litters. The men groan as they are moved on the litter so that Chief Randolph and his assistant can get the necessary views.

The ship rolls and pitches; all the hanging plasma and blood bottles swing with it. The chaplain comforts some of the more sorely distressed. A body is carried out. Litters are tilted up at the foot to improve failing circulations. When a patient is ready for operation, after plasma and blood transfusions and morphine have been administered to relieve shock and raise blood pressure, his clothes are cut off and his wounded parts washed, shaved, and wrapped in clean towels. He is carried off, operated on, and then bedded down in vacated passenger officers' cabins — where the bunks are more convenient and comfortable than those in the compartments in the holds of the ship — or in the sick bay, which is reserved for the most precariously critical since it holds only twenty men.

This purposeful confusion continues as long as there are patients who have not been attended to. Sometimes it is only after thirty-six hours that the mess hall is finally cleared of the last patient. Imagine my physical state then. Now imagine my reaction when at a time like this the familiar order comes over the loudspeaker: "Second Division and medical department stand by to receive casualties."

This train of activity commences all over again and continues until you feel your flesh cannot endure any longer. You want to cry out against the cruelty of it. You want to scream, to go off somewhere where your conscience and body can dissolve into nothingness — to sleep, to forget, to divorce yourself spiritually, physically, from this sort of world, to disown it all. You wonder whether it wouldn't have been better to have stayed home and been a conscientious objector. Every nerve shrieks. Your feet and eyes burn. Your stomach and chest are tight as though in spasm, so that you cannot stand erect and you walk bent over like an old man, and every deep breath tears sore fibers in your lungs. To sit down is not to rest, for there are still so many things to do, and your heart is beating heavily and each pulsation hurts all over your body. A hundred needy jobs flit through your mind. Living hurts.

At long last comes the blessed moment when the mess hall has been cleared of all the candidates for operation, when the mentally and slightly wounded have been carried off to their bunks, when only a body remains — beyond our power to help, awaiting the offices of the chaplain — when my conscience allows me to sneak off to lie down. Even here sleep is a standoffish stranger until I take an amytal tablet to relax my taut nerves.

To awaken after twelve hours of well-earned, unbroken sleep is a wonderful experience, when day and night have both been day for so long. But if you are routed out after only two hours of sleep, you stagger up with the sensation of ants gnawing at every cell in your brain, cursing the broadcast order, "Second Division and medical department stand by to receive casualties." Each time I lay down to sleep I wondered which would be my reaction when I awakened.

Each of the casualties is a picture by El Greco, a novel by Conrad, a poem by the author of Spoon River Anthology. Standing on the lowest step of the ladder, looking down on the rows of dirty faces, I feel that each is a book that has come to the climax of an episode here — the final one for some, a crisis for some, a significant turning point for some. Not one can pass this moment without having his life's current diverted. The course the main character will take from here on is seriously directed by the decisions we doctors must make. The man whose arm or leg I can save by my knowledge or skill has the plot of his novel changed just as surely as the man whose arm or leg I must amputate. The man whose injuries are so serious and extensive that he has practically no chance of surviving any type of treatment, whom Dr. Gil must relegate to the background in order to spend his time on those with less surely fatal wounds — that man too finds Dr. Gil a potent if passing factor in his tale.

Over in the corner, the chaplain is talking to a lad half asleep with morphine, blood running into one arm and plasma into the other. The boy comes from Dr. Gil's home town in Iowa; Dr. Gil knows his father. A piece of shrapnel the size of a walnut tore through his belly wall, through his intestines, through his vertebrae and spinal cord. He has no sensation or power of movement from his waist down. His eyes listlessly watch those moving about him. He will be dead in two hours.

At the far end of the room lies a long, lanky Marine captain, the pallor of death on his cheeks. He can be roused only with difficulty. Both legs are on molded splints, and from one trickles a little stream of bright red blood, forming a pool that undulates with the pitching of the ship. The emergency is great, since the depth of his shock prevents the corpsmen from getting plasma needles into his veins.

Grabbing a scalpel, I cut open his arm, pick up a collapsed vein, tie a needle into it, and get the blood and plasma running into him. A quick look shows that a forty-millimeter shell entered one leg just below the knee and then passed through the opposite calf. He whispers that the shell killed the other five men in the hole with him. One leg will have to come off just above the knee. He needs a quick anesthetic, a tourniquet above both knees, and a fast operation. This captain is a fine man — he got the Navy Cross for bravery at Saipan.

Over here is a man unconscious, with plasma running into his arms. His body, face, and eyes are peppered with thousands of little spots where minute shrapnel fragments penetrated his skin. His belly wall is hard as a rock, so he probably has a peritonitis from perforation of his intestines. Wounded more than twenty-four hours ago, he is too late for operation. We can do no more than carry him along with supportive treatment. One leg is shattered by a dozen large black wounds through which spicules of bone protrude. He moans in his sleep.

Side by side lie three men, all with shattered elbows. Through one elbow there is a hole from front to back made by a shrapnel fragment the size of an olive. Wonder of wonders, although the elbow feels like a loose bag of rough stones and the x-ray shows that the three bones making up the joint are in a hundred pieces, the man has perfect control of his hand, indicating that the vital nerves were not damaged. And the circulation is good.

The second fellow has a wound on the outside of his elbow the size of the sole of your foot, with bones, muscles, cartilage, and arteries all protruding through the hole. I catch a spurting artery with a clamp and tie it off. Although the lateral epicondyle of his humerus has been completely torn off, his radial nerve is still functioning. I wonder about this.

The third has a hunk of metal the size of a pat of butter where his elbow joint used to be. The hand is torn in a dozen places, his kneecap is shattered, and the center of the wound is the size of a teacup. At the upper end of his left thigh is a deep wound an inch in diameter, in the depths of which the x-ray shows a piece of shrapnel shaped like an arrowhead and two inches long. His left testicle has been wounded. He volunteers sleepily, "I got the son of a bitch right between the eyes." I wonder how he did it with all these wounds.

Here is a San Francisco lad. Lord, he must be seven feet tall. White as a sheet. A little hole in the front of his left thigh and a three-inch hole of exit in the rear show the course of the machine-gun bullet that fractured his thigh bone. A nice clean wound like this is easy to fix. A little blood and plasma, a few ties, and some plaster of Paris and I'll fix him slick as a whistle. That wound in the rear makes for swell dependent drainage. Tells me his mother is a nurse, he lives on Monterey Heights, and will I have to take off his leg. "Hell, no. This is one of the easiest things I fix. Nothing I'd rather fix up than a nice compound fracture of the femur."

I look over the wounds of a lad shot in the buttock by a sniper; the bullet came out through a wound in his front belly wall right beside his belly button, tearing his intestines enroute. Here's a case for Dr. Kelly and Dr. Gilfillan. How I hate the thought of these belly cases! Each one takes four hours or more to operate on, and 50 per cent die. Each one takes hours of attention after operation.

In the time that one belly wound is being operated on, I can save half a dozen lives and limbs with other wounds. And I am a lousy belly surgeon. Fortunately, every time we get belly cases, there are other doctors aboard better qualified and always anxious to do them. On one occasion when there were two bellies awaiting operation and it looked as though, willynilly, I should have to do one of them, a man came in with his leg half torn off below the knee and in serious shock. Since this was an emergency, taking precedence even over belly wounds, I had to take him to operation immediately to control his shock and leave the belly to Dr. Gilfillan and Dr. Kelly.

I lift the blanket to look at another man lying quietly. Under the dressings at the upper end of his thighs lie his genitalia, the head of his penis hanging by a thread of tissue, and both testicles out of the sac and exposed like a couple of loops of intestines. Lordy, Lordy, here's another belly, I think, mistaking the testicles for loops of bowel. Looking closer I determine their true nature, to my great relief. We fixed him up swell later, though he lost one testicle and the head of his penis permanently. And his hands were badly torn. It seems that while lying in a shell hole with some of his comrades, he saw a Jap hand grenade coming through the air. He caught it in his hands and it exploded just as its momentum had brought his hands down to the level of his groin. What a man!

Next is brought in a man who needs immediate attention. Covered with volcanic sand and dust, black and dirty, he looks like an exhausted coal-heaver. He is unconscious and in deep shock, and his entire left leg looks like strips of jerky and fresh veal. Nothing resembling a leg remains below six inches from the upper end of his left thigh. An armor-penetrating shell exploded in the lower compartment of his tank, where his leg was resting on the shoulder of his buddy below. Buddy and leg were both blown into shreds.

One of the worthwhile lessons I have learned in the war concerns this type of case. Put him to sleep, apply a high tourniquet, and amputate while resuscitative measures are being employed, not after. You can never get this kind of injury into any sort of decent condition until after the leg has been amputated. So I whacked it off about five inches from the upper end of his thigh. And I had a tough time stopping the bleeding from the bone end, since I didn't have any bone wax along. I finally dammed it off by tamping a vaseline gauze sponge into the bone stump. (Hope someone remembers to take it out.) When I finally unloaded him yesterday, he was pink and smiling and the stump was starting to cover over with skin. He had received the equivalent of six quarts of blood and three of plasma in two weeks.

Since Al Kelly and Dr. Gil were working down in the main surgery, I had set up my bailiwick in the officers' wardroom, where we ship's officers have meals. Passenger officers standing around, waiting orders to go ashore, helped me and my corpsmen by holding limbs and carrying and lifting patients. It must have been a trying experience for the other ship's officers to be eating their meals while on the other side of the room I was debriding wounds, tying bleeders, giving blood transfusions, and amputating limbs under the brilliant and revealing light of the arc lamp.

As soon as patients were ready below, they were carried up the ladder and laid on the unused tables in orderly rows, and like an assembly line, conveyed to my table as I finished with each preceding operation. Dr. Wier and Dr. Gorsuch, two younger medical officers on board just for this campaign, were assisting us or doing dressings in the compartments. Between operations, while the tables and patients were being prepared, I circulated among the untreated casualties below, lining up patients for the receiving end of my assembly line.

A Marine captain came by. Off came one leg. I sweated blood trying to stop bleeding in the gory wound in the center of the calf of the remaining leg, with Dr. Wiener, the dentist-anesthestist, hollering all the while that he could no longer feel any arterial pulse, that the patient was not breathing. "Please do something!" It was a battle. Finally I left four hemostatic clamps protruding from the opening of the wound, packed the gaping hole with vaseline gauze, and wrapped the whole limb in a plaster of Paris cast. I wrote on his clinical chart in the blank after prognosis, "Poor." And did he razz me ten days later when he saw this on the chart. He suggested that I change it to "Favorable," since he was still alive and in good spirits. In the meantime, he had been transfused with blood and plasma equal to twice the volume normally circulating in his body!

Along came a little top sergeant with an arm broken above the elbow by a shrapnel fragment. What a tough time I had with his anesthetic. Pentathol is a wonderful anesthetic for battle cases, but it doesn't mix well in the livers of men who have indulged excessively in bad port and whiskey all their lives. He acted like a wildcat while I was trying to put on the cast. Later, when he was up and around and comfortable in his cast, he was so apologetic. The dentist had given him Hail Columbia for making so much trouble under the anesthetic. He said he hadn't had anything to drink but beer for two years. Of course, before coming into the service he had always had a gallon of port every day, but surely all that had worked out of his system by now. (Sure it had, but not the effect of the alcohol on his liver.)

Here was another lad with his hand torn to mud, blood, clot, bone, and sand. A shrapnel fragment had entered through the middle of his forearm, traveled down the axis of his arm, through his wrist, and then exploded on the back of his hand. What a mess! I had no option but to take off the hand. Some days later when his stump was healing well, he confided to me, "My maw is sure going to be sore about this. Why, when I used to just cut my finger she would go nuts." He didn't seem particularly worried for himself.

A second thigh and leg all torn up. From the middle of the calf down there was no bone remaining in the leg at all. The shell had just squashed out all the bone, leaving skin and muscle hanging like wet red leather strips. There were also great gaping wounds on the thigh, buttock, chest, arm. It was tough work, for it takes lots longer to do a job like this than to tell about it. Coarse, black volcanic sand was ground into all the wound surfaces. Every time I moved him, a shower of sand sifted out of some crevice of his body. Hours seemed to drag by as I got the leg off above the knee, excised all the dirty surfaces of the higher wounds, which were not so deep that they concealed cavities, and then dressed them.

Five days later I came into the cabin where he was bunked with fourteen other seriously injured men to find him and the lad in the next bunk noisy with laughter. He was telling about his operation for appendicitis ten years before, how on the third post-operative day he started to laugh, and laughed and laughed until his belly hurt. This impressed him more than his recent and much graver operation. Just before I sent him off the ship, he told me, his eyes shining with interest, how that day for the first time in the two weeks they had been lying less than three feet apart, he and the man in the bunk below him had been able to look into each other's faces. One of the corpsmen had held up a mirror at an angle which would permit them to exchange glances; neither of them could move yet.

Along came another boy with a multitude of small wounds, none of which was serious, but all of which needed debriding. Holding him by the hand and talking excitedly and affectionately was one of our own crew. They were brothers and were teary with happiness. We put the injured man to sleep and then cleaned him up in a jiffy. Our shipmate in a daze helped the corpsmen carry his quietly sleeping brother away.

And so it goes, day after day. Here's where I check out, folks. You ought to have a picture of the situation by now. Of course, this is only a small corner of the painting, a few hours of these two weeks when I was busy once more and not just sightseeing and diving after South Sea shells. Next time you donate blood to the Red Cross, know that in a few hours it will be flying over the Pacific, and ten thousand miles away some sweating, drooping Doc will soon be pouring it into the veins of an exsanguinated Marine, soldier, or sailor. This refrigerated blood is surely wonderful. It kept alive a lot of fellows who otherwise would not have made the grade. You cannot imagine what a relief it is, in the middle of a tough operation, when the patient is going sour and I am about to go nuts with worry, to be able to save the situation by saying to the corpsman, "Better slip him another quart, Bub."

Respectfully,
Bob

20. Under Way Again

The Doyen's work was almost finished. It was D-day plus fifteen and the land fighting was at last progressing satisfactorily. The American flag had been hoisted on Mount Suribachi, and only that morning we had seen a B-29 land on one of Iwo's air strips. All that remained of Japanese resistance was a pocket of approximately five thousand men holed up in the northern end of the island.

From a naval standpoint the invasion had been easy. Thanks to the activities of our carrier force, only a few planes had managed to break through into the transport area. We saw several of our ships get hit in the distance and witnessed the tremendous bursts of flame sent up. But the attacks were token ones and did not approach the point of effective strength. The only times the Jap planes did come were when the weather was too thick for Allied carrier strikes against the mainland of Japan. What a wonderful feeling it was to be within two air hours of Tokyo and know that the hundreds of planes overhead were our own!

In the relatively close quarters created by the huge armada of ships off the little island of Iwo, there was quite a traffic problem. It was especially hazardous at night, so each evening some of us would retire to cruise about within a radius of twenty miles.

Our larger ships had to keep moving whenever possible. Although most of the Jap batteries were silenced in the first week, enough remained to constitute a threat. One of our ships steamed in close to fire on a pillbox. From out of the mountainside six eight-inch shells crashed into her side, killing and wounding many of her men. The salvo had come from the extreme north end — from a coastal defense gun emplacement that had previously been knocked out.

Oddly enough, the Japs never seemed interested in concentrating their available artillery fire on the transports. Sporadic bursts often fell in the transport area and a couple of ships were hit, but the enemy never seemed to make a real effort. All the while, though, they were carrying on furious artillery and rocket duels with our land force, even though the range was much greater. Whether they had set most of their field pieces to fire in one direction only, or whether they had decided that the troops on the island were of more immediate concern, we never really knew.

On the afternoon of D-day plus fifteen, however, the Japs did get angry at us. About 1400 they sent a flurry of badly aimed shells into our immediate sector. Five of them straddled the Doyen. The junior officer of the deck, Ensign Griffin, excitedly notified Commander Hogan. The commander, busy debarking the last of the troops, snapped back, "Let me know when they hit us." He had barely spoken when an eight-inch shell clipped through our forward boom, knocked off a ventilator, and plunged into the water on the other side. Fortunately it did not explode. There were at least sixty men within ten yards of the area, but the only man hurt was one who dived for a hatch and didn't quite make it. He gashed his head on the metal frame.

That evening our transport squadron was given orders to retire to Guam to discharge casualties. The next morning, after more than two weeks at Iwo, we headed southward.

We stopped for eight hours at Saipan — just long enough to pick up some passengers and give a few of us a chance to go ashore. Four officers went up to the Army base command headquarters to purchase some native souvenirs. When they got to the store, they found they were required to have a letter of authorization from the island commander, since an attempt was being made to regulate prices.

Just as they were about to return empty-handed to the ship, Lieutenant Timmins tried one more approach. Turning to the Chamorro overseer, he told him that our ship had treated a native mother and her little boy. The overseer's expression changed immediately. "Was she wounded in the arm? And was the little boy shot through the stomach?" He took Timmins and led him to the back of the store. There, weaving baskets with her little boy at her side, was the woman who had so much enjoyed our ice cream! The officers got their souvenirs.

On to Guam. It was only a day's trip, but it was not entirely routine. Toward noon a distress signal was picked up by the wireless operator. A badly damaged B-29 was limping home from a raid over Tokyo, and the pilot doubted that he could make it. Ten minutes later we could see the great silver ship in the distance. It was low to the water and dropping rapidly. A moment later the left wing drooped and the plane crashed into the sea. Two of our destroyers rushed to the spot. After several hours word was radioed to the squadron that all the crew members had been saved.

When the information was passed over the loudspeaker, a cheer went up from every member of our crew.

We docked at Guam and discharged our wounded. As soon as the task was completed and our sailing orders were brought aboard, we again headed out to sea.

Where we were going, we did not know. The captain announced that we were heading south to pick up troops for another invasion — in the Ryukyus, it was rumored. "But," he added, "we need a new boom, and our other repair work has reached such a point that this time I feel sure we'll eventually be routed back to the West Coast."

Though the future was in doubt, one thing was certain. Wherever the Doyen went, we would go. She was Attack Transport Number One, and that's where she belonged — at the head of the list. We were proud to be serving   aboard   her.

A NOTE TO THE READER

WE HOPED YOU LOVED THIS BOOK. IF YOU DID, PLEASE LEAVE A REVIEW ON AMAZON TO LET EVERYONE ELSE KNOW WHAT YOU THOUGHT.

WE WOULD ALSO LIKE TO THANK OUR SPONSORS **WWW.DIGITALHISTORYBOOKS.COM** WHO MADE THE PUBLICATION OF THIS BOOK POSSIBLE.

WWW.DIGITALHISTORYBOOKS.COM PROVIDES A WEEKLY NEWSLETTER OF THE BEST DEALS IN HISTORY AND HISTORICAL FICTION.

SIGN UP TO THEIR NEWLSETTER TO FIND OUT MORE ABOUT THEIR LATEST DEALS.

Made in the USA
Lexington, KY
27 May 2019